CONTENTS

Introduction: Beginning With the God Who is
One   xi

**Section A – A Broken World: Scattered Without
God**   1
  1 Eden: Expelled to Wander   5
  2 Babel: Scattered by Pride   18

**Section B – The Assembly of Israel: Gathering
Foreshadowed**   37
  3 Sinai: Gathered Under the Word   41
  4 Jerusalem: Gathered Under the King   66
  5 Babylon: Back to Babel   85

**Section C – The Assembly of Jesus: Gathering
Realized**   105
  6 Golgotha: Gathered to Jesus   107
  7 Pentecost: Gathered by the Spirit   123
  8 Church: Gathered Worldwide   138

**Section D – The New Creation: Gathering
Consummated**   171
  9 The New Creation: Gathered Forever   173

Conclusion: The Glory of the God Who is One   195

    Endnotes   197
    Acknowledgements   201
    ndex of Biblical References   203

Summary Diagram

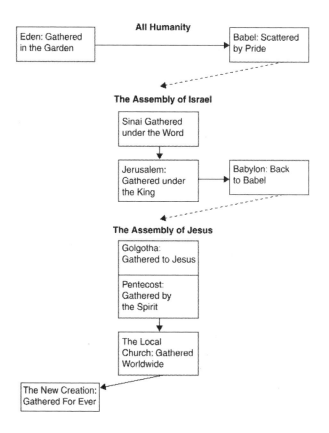

All Humanity

Eden: Gathered in the Garden → Babel: Scattered by Pride

The Assembly of Israel

Sinai Gathered under the Word

Jerusalem: Gathered under the King → Babylon: Back to Babel

The Assembly of Jesus

Golgotha: Gathered to Jesus

Pentecost: Gathered by the Spirit

The Local Church: Gathered Worldwide

The New Creation: Gathered For Ever

To Emmanuel, Wimbledon

Introduction

Beginning With the God Who is One

How is a Broken World to be Remade?

We live in a world that is fractured on every level. From the family to international relations, it is hard to make and maintain harmony. Every day the news brings stories of broken relationships, strife-ridden communities and warring nations. How can it be restored to peace?

The thesis of this little book is that the ordinary local Christian church contains within itself the seeds, or the DNA, of a remade world. That will seem a very surprising thesis to those who think the local church is a complete irrelevance to the real world; and it will be greeted with ironic smiles by those whose experience of local churches is one of strife and tension. But I believe it to be true.

I want to persuade us to commit ourselves whole-heartedly to belonging to, and serving God in the fellowship of, a local church; and that this may prove to be the most significant thing we do with our lives. I want to convince us that the local church is at the heart of the Bible story, that it is close to the heart of the purposes of God, and that it is how a broken world will be remade. I want you to share my passion that the glory of God is inseparably tied up with what happens in the local church.

This message is important in a culture of choice where we are used to being able to shop around for what we want. A recent survey of attitudes amongst non-churchgoers included a positive take on 'spirituality' side by side with a negative attitude to religion. This was compared by one young man to the difference between playing football and being a member of a football team. He was happy with 'spirituality' as a means of fulfilling his personal ambitions (like kicking around a football) but very unhappy at the idea of being constrained by being a committed member of a community (like belonging to a football team). Another commented, 'If I am going to believe in something I will pick my favourite parts of different religions or pick something that I have invented . . . that I feel comfortable with . . . Not what I'm expected to believe in'; another said, 'We take a little bit from this belief and a bit from that, and a bit from the other and then we come to our own major conclusion to live our lives by.'[1] It's all a matter of what I choose.

These personal choice, pick'n'mix attitudes get translated when people become Christians, and they then appear amongst Christians in slightly different clothes. Christians can easily slip into church shopping (finding a church that meets our needs) and church hopping (moving around from church to church without settling into any one). We can get the idea that the Christian life is about special big events and celebrity speakers and find ourselves picky spectators, more interested in evaluating the church experiences on offer than in the hard graft of building deep relationships together shaped by the word of God.

What's the Point of A(nother) Bible Overview?

I want to persuade you, by a grand sweep through the whole Bible, that to belong in a committed and relational way to an ordinary local church may be the most significant thing you do with your life. I am going to try to do that from the whole Bible. That is to say, this book is an overview of the whole Bible story, a shortened and simplified version, an attempt to sum up the Bible story in brief. I live a short bike ride from the British Museum in the heart of London. Sometimes on a day off my wife and I cycle up there for a visit. The British Museum is a huge and fascinating place: it is hard to know where to start. So, in their wisdom, the people who run it offer a 'One Hour Tour' of the museum. They show you some of the highlights, such as the Rosetta Stone and the Parthenon marbles. You can't really begin to see the museum in one hour. But, by taking you round some of the highlights, they hope to whet your appetite to return again and again to explore the treasures.

A Bible overview is a way in to reading the Bible, not a way round. It is like a series of signposts to help us reach a city centre rather than a bypass to make it unnecessary for us to go to the city centre at all. The Bible is greater than the sum of its overviews. You may be familiar perhaps with one overview; I hope you are, because many people have found a Bible overview a helpful way to start finding their way around the Bible. It can give us a sense of how it fits together.

My favourite first overview is *God's Big Picture*, by Vaughan Roberts; this is themed around how the Bible tells the story of the kingdom of God.[2] I have also been greatly helped and stimulated by T. Desmond Alexander's overview, *From Eden to the New Jerusalem*.[3] But because overviews have to choose some governing theme, they all need to omit parts of the Bible that don't tie very closely to that theme. Every Bible overview omits more than it includes. Overviews are like different types of map. One map may highlight physical characteristics such as contours; another may give you the transport networks; a third may focus on political boundaries; a fourth on population density. Each is of value. But the reality of visiting the place will always be greater than the sum of all the maps you can lay your hands on.

Scattering and Gathering

So here's the reason I'm offering you an alternative Bible overview: I want to show you a fresh camera angle on the Bible story, one that brings the local church into sharp focus.

> **This Bible tour focuses on the themes of scattering and gathering: scattering as a sign of God's judgment and gathering as a sign of God's rescue.**

I'm going to tell the Bible story in a way that highlights scattering and gathering. To do that, I will of course miss out a very great deal. Maybe you have seen a photo of a familiar place, but taken from an unfamiliar camera angle or taken with a different kind of lens (perhaps a wide-angle lens rather than a telephoto lens). Perhaps you find yourself looking at a photo of a street you may have known from childhood, and yet noticing things that you have never seen before. No one camera angle or lens will encapsulate the whole experience of living in the street: but they may open our eyes to significant things we had not seen before.

Last summer my wife and I decided to try to learn about wild flowers near the coast in South Wales where we were on holiday. Armed with our pocket guide to wild flowers, we set out. Before long, we spotted our first Viper's Bugloss. But having spotted one, it wasn't long before we were seeing these lovely little wild flowers all over the place. I am so unobservant I had never seen them before at all, though I must have walked by hundreds of them. My hope is that this distinctive Bible overview will open our eyes to the significance of the local church.

Incidentally, this camera angle is not necessarily any better or worse than other camera angles. People sometimes ask how we can know whether a particular Bible overview is 'the right one'. The answer is: they all are and none of them is, though some are more valuable than others. Imagine a photographer taking a photograph of a great sculpture for an illustrated book. No camera angle would be wrong, but some might show off the sculpture better than others. The test is whether or not a photo gives readers a good two-dimensional 'feel' for the majesty of the three-dimensional statue. You will have to judge to what extent the scattering and gathering theme gives us an overall grasp of the Bible story.

Beginning with the God Who is One

Let us start with God. A famous Christian of the fourth century wrote that, 'the very best order of . . . every speech and action, is to begin from God and to end in God'.[4] He was right: we shall start and end our story with God.

The Lord our God, the Lord is One

Our starting text is one of the most famous verses in the Bible:

Hear, O Israel: The LORD our God, the LORD is one. (Deut. 6:4)

This is the famous 'Shema' recited regularly in synagogues for centuries. ('Shema' is the Hebrew word for 'Hear!' or 'Listen!'). Moses is preaching to the people of God just before they moved into the Promised Land. There are just four Hebrew words in the statement he makes: The-LORD our-God the-LORD One (In Hebrew, 'the LORD' is one word, as is 'our God'). 'The LORD' in capital letters in our English translations is sometimes written 'Yahweh' or 'Jehovah'; it is the Hebrew name of the God of the Bible. He is the God of Abraham, Isaac, and Jacob, the God of Moses and of the Exodus. He is the God who makes a covenant (or agreement) with his people. The strapline of the Covenant is, 'You will be my people and I will be your God' (e.g. Exod. 6:7 or Ezek. 36:28). Moses calls him 'our God', not because he is the private god of Israel (as if there were lots of other valid gods and goddesses) but because he is the God who is in covenant relationship with Israel.

The emphasis and climax of the statement is the word 'one': the God of the Bible story, the covenant God in relationship with us, is *one*! This is a huge statement; it is rather like a part of a website that is full of hyperlinks elsewhere; it connects all over the Bible story. This is not a simple mathematical oneness that would stop God being Father, Son and Holy Spirit, one God in Trinity, as we shall see in Chapter 7 (e.g. 1 Cor. 8:6). So what does it mean?

1. One God

First, it means that the God of the Bible is the only real God. Centuries later the apostle Paul wrote to the church in Corinth, 'We know that an idol is nothing at all in the world and that there is no God but one' (1 Cor. 8:4). The words, 'is nothing at all in the world' mean that an idol 'has no real existence' (ESV). Of course, a god or goddess such as a Hindu god or the Muslim Allah exists, in a sense; but they exist only in the imaginations of their worshippers. They do not have any substantial, objective existence independent of the minds and hearts of their worshippers. If their worshippers ceased to worship them, they would cease to exist. Only the God of the Bible exists independently of us: we could cease to exist and yet he would still exist. His divinity and reality would be unaffected.

2. One reality

Second, this verse therefore means that there is only one objective and substantial reality in the universe. This may sound rather philosophical, but it is important. I remember listening to a young woman called Julia telling her story. Julia had been brought up in a Christian home and had then gone to study Geography at university. There she had been immersed in a world-view in which it was firmly and repeatedly asserted that there is 'no one reality'. There is 'my reality' and there is 'your reality'. 'Your reality' may be real and true in a subjective sense 'for you'; and yet 'my reality' (which may contradict 'your reality') can still be true or real 'for me'. In the intellectual world where Julia studied it was insisted upon (yes, really insisted upon, as if *this* truth were somehow really true!) that there is no one reality that is real in the whole world.

This is a world many of us inhabit at school or university or in the workplace. Not surprisingly Julia said she became confused, because a world with no one reality is a very confusing place. It was not until she found her rest in the one real God that her confusion was replaced by clarity. One true God means that there is one objective substantial reality within which you and I have to live. We can create our subjective or virtual quasi-realities as much as we like, but the day will come when we must reckon with what one theologian called, 'The God who is there', and therefore with the reality that is there.[5]

3. One morality

Third, a consequence of this is that there is one objective morality: there is such a thing as right and such a thing as wrong; morality is objectively true and not subjectively relative. By and large our culture does not accept this. The writer Will Self described the cultural world of his childhood like this: he was brought up in 'a world where ethics, so far from inhering in the very structure of the cosmos, was a matter of personal taste akin to a designer label, sewn into the inside lining of conscience'.[6] It is a vivid image: you choose your ethics label, and I choose mine, but it is no more than a matter of personal taste.

Taken to its logical conclusion, this is a frightening world, in which a paedophile or serial killer can claim that they are following their own personal moral code, and who are we to say they are objectively wrong? However, in the poetic language of the Old Testament, the world is not like a chaotic sea, with right and wrong shifting wildly from side to side in the waves. Instead it is firmly placed on pillars or foundations, a secure moral order rooted in the reality of the God who is One. For example, when Hannah the mother of the prophet

Samuel celebrates the justice of God she sings, 'For the *foundations* of the earth are the LORD's; upon them he has set the world' (1 Sam. 2:8). That is, in Will Self's words, right and wrong do inhere 'in the very structure of the cosmos.'

4. Harmony under one ruler

Finally, all this means that there ought to be universal harmony under one ruler. The world is a coherent place because it is made and sustained by one real God. It is not the playground or battlefield of many gods and goddesses all competing for supremacy, vying for the superior places in the heavenly Cabinet chamber. This is very different from the world of animism, in which we are at the mercy of the spirits of trees, of rivers, and of mountain tops. It is very different from the world of the Greek and Roman pantheons which formed the culture of the New Testament world around the Mediterranean Sea. It is very different from the thousands of Hindu gods and goddesses. The world is not like Iraq after the toppling of Saddam Hussein, a country riven with competing people groups, or the Balkans after Marshall Tito, disintegrating into warring regions like Bosnia, Serbia, Kosovo, and Croatia. Nor is it like an anarchic school playground where the teachers are absent and life is one long fight for survival and supremacy.

The Bible story in three acts

But here's the problem: the world quite clearly is not living in harmony under one ruler. It is all too much like an anarchic playground. The Bible recognizes precisely this tension. The clearest echo of the Shema in the Old Testament comes right near the end of Israel's history before Christ. After the exile in Babylon, the prophet Zechariah looks forward to a future day when, 'the LORD will be king over all the earth. On that day the LORD will be one and his name one'.[7]

In many places the Bible asserts that God is already king over all the earth. For example, he is 'the LORD Most High, the great King over all the earth' (Ps. 47:2). So how can Zechariah look forward to a future day when he '*will be* king over all the earth' if he is already king? Or, to put it another way, how can the Bible assert so firmly that the LORD is one and at the same time look forward to a day when the LORD will be one (Deut. 6:4; Zech. 14:9)? I think the answer is in the parallel statement in Zechariah: 'and his *name* one'. His 'name' speaks not just of his identity but also of his reputation, of human beings acknowledging his kingship. In one sense, he is king over the whole earth now but, in another sense, he isn't. In one sense, he is 'one' now but, in another sense, he isn't. He is king in the sense that he governs the world exactly as he pleases: he is the Sovereign Lord. And he is 'one' in the sense that his reality and glory undergirds creation. But he is not universally acknowledged ('named') and known as the one true God. His world is peopled by rebels who are governed by God despite their hostility and against their will. Zechariah looks forward to that great day when the renewed creation will be governed by God through a redeemed humanity who will gladly bow the knee and praise him. But we are jumping ahead to the end of the story.

The story of the Bible is the story of how God will bring about that great day. The Bible may be thought of as a story in three acts. Act I is very brief, because it lasts only until Genesis 3. We might call Act I 'Harmony'. God makes one coherent creation, a universe in which his will is done perfectly and without complexity equally in 'heaven' (God's space) and on 'earth' (our space-time universe); there is no curtain or barrier between God's space ('heaven') and our space ('earth').

Act II may be called 'Fracture', and it lasts from Genesis 3 until near the end of the book of Revelation. In Act II, although God continues to be the sovereign ruler of the universe, his will is not done on 'earth' in the same way as it is done in 'heaven' (which is why we must pray in the Lord's Prayer, 'Your will be done on earth as it is in heaven' (Matt. 6:10)). Now it is a case of, 'God is in heaven and you are on earth; so let your words be few' (Eccl. 5:2). Because human beings break away from God's loving rule and decide to live their lives without reference to the God who made them, the whole universe is put out of joint, and humanity becomes fractured and scattered. Fault lines appear all over the place, and men and women are at war with one another and misgoverning a world that cries out to be well-governed. The world is a broken place because it is alienated from God who made it.

And yet the God who made it has not given up on it. He is at work to remake the world he still loves. God is determined not to be defeated. He will win, and his victory will see his world remade as he intended it to be. This is why Act III is 'The New Creation', the new heavens and new earth (i.e. the renewed and restored universe), which is pictured for us in apocalyptic language at the end of the book of Revelation.

However, a Bible overview that simply divided the Bible storyline into three parts like this would not be very helpful to Bible readers. It would put less than 1 per cent into Act I and Act III and leave over 99 per cent of the Bible in Act II! So I am going to shape our tour around nine critical Bible places or events on the way.

The Bible story in nine places

Our Bible tour is going to start in Eden, and then pause at Babel, Sinai, Jerusalem, Babylon, Golgotha, Pentecost, and Church, before concluding in the New Creation.

We are going to begin in the garden in Eden, with harmony, the nucleus of a gathered humanity close to God. We shall see that harmony tragically broken, and pause at the iconic story of the Tower of Babel in Genesis 11 to see the fractured world vividly pictured for us. The movement from Eden to Babel speaks of a world that is scattered and fractured because it is alienated from the creator God who is One.

From Babel we will fast-forward through the promises God made to Abraham, Isaac, and Jacob, and the great rescue of God's people from Egypt (the Exodus), to Mount Sinai where the Ten Commandments and the Law of Moses were given. At Sinai the people of God assemble by the mountain under God's spoken word of law: we shall see in this rabble gathered at the mountain the foreshadowing of a remade world. From Sinai we move to Jerusalem, to see how the foreshadowed remaking of the world develops with the promises of God's king given to David. Jerusalem becomes a powerful symbol of a regathered world.

From Jerusalem, however, we must move to Babylon, a word which came to symbolize the scattering of God's people in exile. The historical Babylon became much more than a place; it became a reprise of all the scattering that the ancient Tower of Babel symbolized. By the time we have travelled from Eden through Babel, Sinai, and Jerusalem and then out to Babylon, we really do not seem to have made any progress. What kind of a story is it that spends so long getting us from Babel to Babylon?

It becomes clear that Sinai and Jerusalem together are not the remaking of a broken world, but rather the foreshadowing and anticipation of the actual remaking, which is yet to come.

The story continues after Babylon until we come to the central event of human history, at Golgotha, the place of the Skull (the place where Jesus was crucified) (Matt. 27:33). This terrible unfair death, itself the epitome of what goes wrong in a broken world, turns out paradoxically to be the event around which a remade world will focus and the magnet which will draw all sorts of people together. From Golgotha we move to the first Christian Pentecost in Jerusalem, where the miraculous understanding of different human languages signifies the reversal of the babble of tongues that was Babel. Golgotha and Pentecost show us how the promises of gathering in the Old Testament will finally be made real in the church.

So from Pentecost we move to the local church, which is at the same time scattered all over the world and yet contains within itself the seeds of a worldwide gathering – local churches are scattered gatherings! We shall spend some time exploring how a local church is shaped around themes from Sinai and Jerusalem, while still suffering from being placed in a world east of Eden and in the long shadow of the Tower of Babel. We shall look at how the local church is made possible by the Cross and the gift of the Holy Spirit. Finally, from the scattered gathering that is the local church we follow the trajectory of grace to end our story with the New Jerusalem, a picture of the renewed Creation, a broken world remade at last to the glory of the God who is One. It is a great story.

Questions for Discussion

1. Review what this chapter teaches about God. Why does the nature of God mean there ought to be harmony in the world?
2. Why does it matter so much that there should be harmony in the world?
3. What experiences do you have of the pain of a broken world? What behaviours have caused this brokenness?
4. What experiences do you have of relationships in a local church? Do people relate differently there, or not?

is a church in which God gathers his people and meets with them together. No wonder it was a day they never forgot! We need to remember when we gather in the local church that our assemblies are not just functional (to encourage us in our Christian lives); they are the reason God has redeemed us. He longs to have his people gathered to him and therefore to one another, because only then will they be the sign and foretaste of a remade world.

B. God assembles all his people

Notice next that the Assembly at Sinai was the gathering of *all* God's people. Again and again in Deuteronomy, Moses addresses 'all Israel' and expects future gatherings to be of 'all Israel' (e.g. Deut. 1:1; 5:1; 31:1 and e.g. Deut. 31:11). This theme continues in Israel's history and is especially emphasized by the writer of 1 and 2 Chronicles (e.g. 1 Chr. 13:5). As the numbers grew, and when they were spread out in the Promised Land, it was not physically possible for every Israelite to assemble, and there must have been times when 'all Israel' was a meeting of the senior representatives of Israel.

But the expression 'all Israel' conveys a very important theological truth, which is that there is one people of God belonging to the one God. The God who is One must have one people: he cannot, by definition, have lots of separated and divided peoples. There is a distinction between Israel and the Gentiles, but there is to be no distinction within Israel; there are not to be two or more 'Israels' (although, as we shall see, that is precisely what happened in Israel's history).

In our terms, there is to be a distinction between the church and the world; but there are not to be many separated churches. Of course, all over the physical world now there are different assemblies: but theologically there is one people of God, not many. The local church is to be the local expression of the whole people of God. This means that no local church should be deliberately particular or exclusive in the way it restricts itself to any one subset of the people of God, by gender (a church for men or a church for women), by race (a black church, a white church, a yellow church), by age (a church for the young, a church for the old), or by culture (a church for professionals, a church for the working class).

Having said this, we must remember that every church is built in the long shadow of the Tower of Babel. Language barriers are the most obvious manifestation of this: every church has to decide which language a meeting will be conducted in. And beyond this, all manner of cultural barriers are expressions of broader forms of language barriers. We joke the British and the Americans are separated by a common language, and the same is true of all sorts of people within Britain or within America. We may speak the same language at one level, but all sorts of markers, idioms, and accents within that language still serve to divide, as they do with every country. A church cannot avoid having some culture expressed in the way it meets and behaves; because of the fragmentation of human society, every church will inevitably reflect something of the specifics of where it is located: but every authentic church will begin to dilute, break down and undermine as many barriers as they can, as all the people of God are gathered by God's call.

C. God assembles that we may hear and obey his voice

God gathers by speaking. God said to Moses, 'Assemble the people before me *to hear my words* . . .' (Deut. 4:10). Not only is the assembly called together by the command of God, it is also gathered in order that they should hear and heed the word of God. The reason they gathered was not to look, but to listen. Moses stresses this:

> Remember the day you stood before the LORD your God at Horeb, when he said to me, "Assemble the people before me to hear my words so that they may learn to revere me as long as they live in the land and may teach them to their children." You came near and stood at the foot of the mountain while it blazed with fire to the very heavens, with black clouds and deep darkness. *Then the LORD spoke to you out of the fire. You heard the sound of words but saw no form; there was only a voice.* He declared to you his covenant, the Ten Commandments, which he commanded you to follow and then wrote them on two stone tablets. And the LORD directed me at that time to teach you the decrees and laws you are to follow in the land that you are crossing the Jordan to possess. *You saw no form of any kind the day the LORD spoke to you* at Horeb out of the fire. (4:10–15)

Of course there were some things they saw: they saw the mountain burning with fire, they saw a deep darkness and cloud. But if you asked them later what they had seen, they would have said, 'I don't really know what I saw, it had no shape or form, but I know exactly what I heard. I heard his voice. I heard the Covenant, the Ten Commandments.' Sinai was not so much a wonderful sight, as an awesome and clear sound.

This teaches us that the reason we gather in church is first that we may hear and submit to the voice of God in his word. He assembles us by his command, and we assemble to listen to his word. The word of God is the driving force that shapes authentic church life. This is why the primacy of preaching and Bible teaching is not just one tradition amongst other equally valid Christian traditions: it is the defining mark of the assembly of the people of God. Unless our first desire when we gather is to hear and heed the voice of God in his word, we have missed the foundation point of church.

D. Our relationships are to be shaped by the law of God so we can live together in peace

Only the word of God brings us together, and only the word of God can keep us together in harmony. The word of God is not an arbitrary exercise of God's authority, like God throwing his weight around to make sure we treat him with respect! The law of God is the only way of living that can enable human beings to live in peace. Unless our assemblies are shaped by the law of God they will never stay assembled.

What precisely they heard at Sinai was the Ten Commandments. The LORD 'declared to you his Covenant, the Ten Commandments, which he commanded you to follow and then wrote them on two stone tablets' (Deut. 4:13). The Ten Commandments stand on their own level as the direct law of God, spoken unmediated by the voice of God at Sinai and written, as it were, directly by the finger of God on tablets of stone (a vivid way of speaking about them as directly from God himself) (9:10). They are put in the Ark (box) of the Covenant and sum up the covenant relationship between God and his people (10:5). Moses then expanded and applied these great commandments in detail to the corporate life of Israel: 'And the LORD directed me at that time to teach you the decrees and laws you are to follow in the land that you are crossing the Jordan to possess' (4:14). What Moses calls here 'the decrees and laws' are all the other laws.

The purpose of all these laws is to shape a people who will live in harmony with God, at peace with one another, and govern God's world properly. That is to say, they are to shape a people who will remake a broken world. It is helpful to begin to flesh this out by considering briefly the great principles of the Ten Commandments one by one (Exod. 20:1–17; Deut. 5:6–21).

1. Only one God: In a world of many gods, they are to love the God who is One with undivided loyalty. This alone can unite society in joyful true worship.
2. No idols: In a world that loves to reshape god in our own image (what I think God ought to be like), they are to worship him only as he has revealed himself. This will prevent the terrible divisiveness of human religion inventing god in all sorts of different human images (and then fighting over which of our images is right).
3. Honouring the name of God: In a world that takes God very lightly, they are to honour his 'name', that is his revealed character, treating him with reverence. This is the antidote to the pride of Babel.
4. Sabbath rest: In an anxious and driven world which prides itself on working 24/7 and cannot risk resting (or letting others rest) they are to rejoice in rhythms of work and rest, trusting in the sufficiency of God so that their prosperity does not depend entirely on them. This will enable them to create a society which is generous in allowing others to rest (see especially the way Moses preaches this commandment in Deut. 5:12–15).
5. Honouring parents: The command to honour parents stands in the Ten Commandments as a shorthand for respecting all the God-given structures of human authority, since the family is the core and foundation

of those structures. To respect authority will prevent society disintegrating into anarchy and chaos, which is why it comes with the promise ('that you may live long in the land . . .' (Exod. 20:12 and see also Eph. 6:2)).

6. No murder: In a world full of hatred and anger, they are to learn to shun any behaviour that harms or desires to harm another human being. Instead they are to love their neighbours as themselves (Lev. 19:18).

7. No adultery: In an unfaithful world, they are to learn to value sexual faithfulness in the covenant of marriage, and to flee from sexual intimacy in all other contexts. Their society will then be saved from the miserable jealousies and discontent of sexual chaos.

8. No stealing: In an unjust world, they are to learn to hate stealing and unjust business dealings. Instead, they are to learn to love generosity, to work that they may have something to share and give, because they know the God who richly gives us all things to enjoy (Eph. 4:28 and 1 Tim. 6:17).

9. No false witness: In a deceitful world they are to hate false witness, which means lying for our gain and another's harm. They are to love truth, because they know the God who is faithful and true.

10. No covetousness: In a self-obsessed world, they are to learn to hate greed and covetousness because they are learning to trust the God who has said, 'I will never leave you nor forsake you' (Heb. 13:5). In this way their society can be harmonious and preserved from the miseries of envious covetousness, always looking over our shoulders to see what kind of husband or wife, what kind of job, what kind of house, what kind of holidays and leisure, other people have got.

Only an assembly shaped by this good law will live together in harmony. This law alone is the relational pattern that makes for peace. A society shaped by these principles will live together in peace and not be scattered by strife: it will remake a broken world.

E. If we shape our own gods we will go back to Babel

Moses sets before the assembly a simple but very deep choice: either they are shaped by the voice of God and stay gathered, or they shape themselves any way they want and will end up scattered. The great burden of his sermon in Deuteronomy 4 is to warn them of the disastrous results of idolatry.

> You saw no form of any kind the day the LORD spoke to you at Horeb out of the fire. *Therefore watch yourselves very carefully, so that you do not become corrupt and make for yourselves an idol*, an image of any shape, whether formed like a man or a woman, or like any animal on earth or any bird that flies in the air, or like any creature that moves along the ground or any fish in the waters below. And when you look up to the sky and see the sun, the moon and the stars – all the heavenly array – do not be enticed into bowing down to them . . .' (vv. 15–19)

To make an idol was precisely what they had done at Sinai. While Moses was up the mountain, we read:

> When the people saw that Moses was so long in coming down from the mountain, they gathered [assembled] round Aaron and said, "Come, make us gods who will go before us . . ." (Exod. 32:1)

And so the golden calf was made, shaped by Aaron to reflect the kind of religion they wanted, which was pretty much the same kind of human-centred religion of all the peoples round about, god in the shape we want god to be.

However, they are not to imagine that they can shape and mould God into their own likeness, to make an idol in the shape they want. Either the assembly is shaped by the word of God spoken to them from above, from outside their own hearts and imaginations, or it will be shaped by the desires and imaginations of their own hearts. The broken world will not be remade by human beings gathering together by their own initiative and deciding what they think God ought to be like, for then he will always be a pale reflection of their own culture, and thus always in conflict with other humanly-shaped gods from other cultures. It will only be remade by the sovereign word of God preached to them from outside, over which they have no control and to which they must submit.

For years in my Christian life I thought idolatry in the Bible was what the appendix is in the human body – a relict of some bygone age when no doubt it had a purpose, but not now; leave it out and you won't miss it. There are many evils in the world of which I need to beware, from which I need to guard myself, but surely idolatry is so laughable that I am safe from *that*, I thought. There is an old hymn which began, 'From Greenland's icy mountains, From India's coral strand . . .' It is about the moral darkness of the rest of the world, in which, in the words of verse two, 'The heathen in his blindness, bows down to wood and stone.' But not us! Some time ago, I read in the paper a sculptor in Thailand had added a gold-plated statue of David Beckham to a Buddhist temple in Bangkok, alongside various other minor deities. And of course we laugh. 'How absurd!' we say.

In his autobiography *Father and Son*, the nineteenth-century writer Edmund Gosse describes an experiment he carried out as a six year old. He had heard his godly parents speak of the terrible sin of idolatry; he asked his father what this was and was told that idolatry consisted in praying to any one or anything but God alone. In particular 'Wood and stone were particularly liable to be bowed down to by the heathen in their blindness.' Being assured by his father that this sin made God very angry, and that God would signify his anger, the rebellious boy determined to try an experiment.

> I determined . . . to test the matter for myself, and one morning, when both my parents were safely out of the house, I prepared for the great act of heresy. I was in the morning-room on the ground-floor, where, with much labour, I hoisted a small chair on to the table close to the window.
>
> My heart was now beating as if it would leap out of my side, but I pursued my experiment. I knelt down on the carpet in front of the table, and looking up I said my daily prayer in a loud voice, only substituting the address 'O Chair!' for the habitual one.
>
> Having carried this act of idolatry safely through, I waited to see what would happen. It was a fine day, and I gazed up at the slip of white sky above the houses opposite, and expected something to appear in it. God would certainly exhibit his anger in some terrible form, and would chastise my impious and wilful action . . . [but nothing happens, and he concludes] I had committed idolatry, flagrantly and deliberately, and God did not care.[34]

But it's such a trivial mistake. Edmund Gosse was an idolater, but not in the way he considered here. He assumed that idolatry was an outward action. And yet the Bible makes clear that idolatry is a matter of the heart. The physical bowing down to an image of wood or stone is but one symptom of the disease of the heart. In two of his letters Paul speaks of greed or covetousness as being idolatry (Eph. 5:5; Col. 3:5). At the end of his first letter John suddenly – out of the blue it seems – ends with the stark words, 'Dear children, keep yourselves from idols' – full stop, end of letter (1 John 5:21). So what is idolatry, if it is not just the physical making of an image of a god? In his letter to the church in Rome, Paul says that idolatry means to exchange the truth about God for a lie and to give our worship to things that have been made, rather than to the one creator God (Rom. 1:23–25). The point about idolatry is this. You and I – and the animals and birds etc – are created. God is the creator. He made us; we did not make him. He made us human beings in his image, to be like him.

To be an idolater is to turn it upside down, to exchange the creator for the created. So that I – as a created being – put myself in the place of the creator and make for myself a god fashioned in my image, created and shaped by me, chosen by me, so that this is the god of my shaping and my choosing. So although I claim to worship it, in fact it is me who is firmly in control. For if I choose to reshape my god, who is to stop me? I made it; I can remake it. He, she or it is my project, my ambition, my decision.

Human beings are made to worship. We must bow down and serve some god, some cause, some project or some reason for living; we've got to have someone or something to serve; otherwise we'll just roll over on our backs and stick our feet in the air like a dead beetle! As Martin Luther said, 'If a man will not have God, he must have his idols.' We create our idols all the time when we will not worship God. The Reformer John Calvin said, 'the human heart is a factory of idols'; we're always creating new models. It may be a new form of greed. It may be an obsession with success in my career. It may be I make my family into an idol, so that feathering my nest and building up my little nuclear family becomes my big goal, and all my time and all my money is poured into this little family, and woe betide anybody who suggests I might have wider obligations in God's world. We make many idols.

The point at Sinai is not that the LORD was invisible whereas idols are visible. It is not that the LORD is spiritual whereas idols are physical. No, it is that idols are visible but the LORD was *audible*. The difference is profound, because it is the difference of who is in control. You see, says Moses, we saw no form: we do not know what God looks like, we do not know his shape. So if we make a shape or image it will tell you everything about us and our desires and nothing about God and his character.

But when God speaks it is different: for what he says is not an echo of what is in my heart. He does not rubber stamp my longings when he speaks. I do not choose what he says. He does not speak in the misquoted 'still small voice' inside me, for this so-called voice is a subjective creation of my own complex psyche.[35] No, he speaks objectively in words that come to you and me from outside ourselves. He is in control. He speaks and my duty is to hear and obey. I may or may not find what he says congenial or comfortable, but he speaks.

Let me share with you an analogy which I think helps to make this distinction clear. In his very personal testimony, *A Grief Observed*, C.S. Lewis speaks of what it is to live on after the death of his beloved wife. One of the things he says – and I think this is very profound – is about memory. He speaks of the shallow way people say, 'She will live forever in your memory.' But he points out that this is utter rubbish. '*Live?* That is exactly what she won't do.' And the reason she won't live in his memory is that in his memory she is an image who will do whatever he wants. A remembered image 'will smile or frown, be tender, gay, ribald, or argumentative just as your mood demands. It is a puppet of which you hold the strings.' But in life she had not been like that. She was another and she chose whether to smile or frown, and so on.[36]

The opposite of idolatry is true worship. The living God is *other* to us. He lives, he speaks, he chooses, he acts, and we respond. By contrast, an idol is an image which does our bidding. That's why real worship is so dangerous: to gather around the word of God and to take seriously what the living God says objectively to us – it's a dangerous adventure. It is possible to go through all the motions of Christian religion and be an idolater: because the so-called 'God' we say we worship is actually made in our image: he fits into our tramlines, our box, and does just what we expect him to do. This is why it is so important, says Moses, to submit to his word, for the people of God to be gathered in expectancy under the word of God.

Moses goes on in Deuteronomy 4 to spell out why idolatry matters so deeply. The main thrust of verses 20 to 24 is the jealousy of God. God is a jealous lover who absolutely insists that his beloved should be his and his alone. This is a good jealousy. It is the jealousy any married person ought to feel, and God feels it for his people, who are his bride. The Covenant is the binding obligation of exclusive mutual love and loyalty.

Idolatry is playing with fire. God's jealous love is like a holy fire which burns with settled and furious anger against infidelity. We must bow down and worship him alone. Idolatry matters because it is a breach of trust. It is infidelity. It is terribly serious. It leads to helpless scattering.

> After you have had children and grandchildren and have
> lived in the land a long time – if you then become corrupt
> and make any kind of idol, doing evil in the eyes of the
> LORD your God and provoking him to anger, I call heaven
> and earth as witnesses against you this day that you will
> surely perish from the land that you are crossing the Jordan
> to possess. You will not live there long but will certainly be
> destroyed. *The LORD will scatter you* among the peoples, and
> only a few of you will survive among the nations to which
> the LORD your God will drive you. There you will worship
> man-made gods of wood and stone, which cannot see or
> hear or eat or smell. (Deut. 4:25–28)

An idolatrous people end up corrupt, scattered, and
defeated. They cry out to the gods they have shaped, and
find that those gods have no eyes, ears or power to help
them. The whole problem with an idol is because I made
it, it has no power beyond me to help me when I am in
need. Idolatry is such a cruel delusion. It is all about
image: an idol is like a marketing brand. Like a brand, an
idol is very vulnerable to being shown up when it comes
face to face with reality. There was a famous advertising
copywriter in the 1920s called Helen Woodward who
warned anyone writing an advertisement *not* to visit the
factory in which the product was made. For, she said,
'when you know the truth about anything, the real inner
truth – it is very hard to write the surface fluff which sells
it.'[37] When idolatry comes face to face with suffering and
pain it is shown up for the dead sham that it is. No-one
facing a terminal illness says, 'I wish I had passed more
exams, I wish I had spent more hours in the office, I wish
I had got more promotions, I wish I had earned more

money, I wish I had followed the lifestyle magazines more slavishly, I wish I had owned more . . .'

Some years ago the little toddler Jamie Bulger was abducted and murdered by two ten-year-old boys in Liverpool. The crime provoked widespread questioning about our society. One national newspaper proclaimed in a headline, 'All our gods have failed.' That was true. When a society worships success, technology, power or wealth, and then finds moral decay in its midst, to whom can we turn? Will our careers save us? Will our wealth save us? Can technology bring moral order out of moral decay? All those gods have failed and will always fail.

One of the main lessons we learn from Sinai is gathering is only possible when God does it, and when the people who are gathered submit to the word of God and allow their relationships to be shaped by it. Whenever we shape gods to suit our own desires we end up scattered, back at Babel.

The problem is that ancient Israel were at heart still idolaters, and Moses knows it. The sad irony is that they continued to shape their own gods: and they did end up back in Babel.

F. The Sinai church is an assembly at a distance

So far in our study of Sinai we have not dwelt on one of the most striking features of this assembly. It may be a wonderful thing to see the first God-called church east of Eden, but it has a very different feel from those wonderful days in the garden before Adam's disobedience.

There, the LORD walked in the garden and spoke with his gardeners as with his friends. Here, he descends from heaven to the top of the mountain in fire, darkness, gloom and storm, speaking words so terrifying the people begged him to stop and let Moses be their mediator and God's spokesman. If even an animal touched the mountain while God was on the top of it, the animal had to be killed from a distance by arrows or stoning: anyone who touched a creature that had touched the sacred mountain would be killed.

The writer of the New Testament 'Letter to the Hebrews' (i.e. to Jewish Christians) describes that day as coming

> . . . to a mountain that can be touched [that is, a darkness so thick you could metaphorically touch it] and that is burning with fire; to darkness, gloom and storm; to a trumpet blast or to such a voice speaking words that those who heard it begged that no further word be spoken to them, because they could not bear what was commanded: "If even an animal touches the mountain, it must be stoned." The sight was so terrifying that Moses said, "I am trembling with fear." (12:18–21)

What a frightening assembly, what a terrifying church to come to! It was not an assembly for access to God, but rather an assembly in which they had to keep their distance from God. This paradox signals to us the gateway into Eden is still guarded by the cherubim and flaming sword (Gen. 3:24). These angels were like God's bouncers, preventing human beings from re-entering Eden. It is going to be no light matter to remake a broken world, for human beings with rebellious hearts will be burned up by the fire of God's holiness if they come into his presence. In words echoed in the New Testament, Moses says to them that, 'the LORD your God is a consuming fire, a jealous God' (Deut. 4:24; Heb. 12:29). To say he is 'a jealous God' simply means he must have our complete and wholehearted loyalty: we cannot 'two-time' God by having an affair with other gods, and still live; he is the all or nothing God. That is the inevitable consequence of God being One. He cannot just stand down his bouncers, say he's changed his mind and feels he's been a bit tough on Adam and Eve, and just let us back into the garden. The moral coherence of the universe would disintegrate if he did that without our rebellion being atoned for.

And yet unless we are brought back into his presence we cannot live in harmony with one another or with the created order. So what is to be done? This tension lies beneath that great day at Sinai, and all the law given then. Moses' sermon in Deuteronomy 4 ends not with human failure but with God's promise, the promise of a remade world. Looking ahead to days of exile, Moses concludes,

> When you are in distress and all these things have happened to you, then in later days you will return to the LORD your God and obey him. For the LORD your God is a merciful God; he will not abandon you or forget the covenant with your forefathers, which he confirmed to them by oath. (vv. 30,31)

It is a relief to know the letter to the Hebrews, in the passage quoted above, says that Christian people have *not* come to Mount Sinai in our churches (Heb. 12:18)! So although we learn important lessons about submission to the word of God, thank God there are some wonderful differences between the Sinai church and church today.

Questions for Discussion

1. Review what happened between Babel and Sinai. In what ways had God's promise of remaking a broken world begun, and in what ways not yet?

2. What new thing happened at Sinai?
3. Think carefully about your local church meetings. In what ways is the life of your local church shaped and driven by listening to the voice of God through the Bible?
4. How do you think we shape God to be the way we would like him to be? In particular, how can we find ourselves using the Bible to make God seem the way we would like him to be?
5. Are there projects or people in church life that become so important to us that we are in danger of making them into idols? How can we avoid this?

4

Jerusalem: Gathered Under the King

We ended the last chapter by noting the letter to the Hebrews says that Christians have *not* come to Mount Sinai when they assemble. This is why we drew lines from only some of the pattern of Sinai to the church, but not all. The writer goes on to say, 'But you *have* come to Mount Zion, to the heavenly Jerusalem . . .' (Heb. 12:22). He is speaking in symbolic terms, and we shall see in Chapter 9 what he means by 'the heavenly Jerusalem'. To help us understand the heavenly Jerusalem, we need first to see the significance of the earthly Jerusalem in Old Testament times.

From Sinai to Jerusalem

The journey from Sinai to Jerusalem took centuries. First there was a 40-year wandering in the desert (Num. 10:11 – 36:13, summarized by Moses in Deut. 1:19 – 3:29). Then the book of Deuteronomy records Moses' final preaching to the people on the edge of the Promised Land. The book of Joshua records the invasion and settlement of the land. The book of Judges recounts how Israel was governed (or 'judged') for many years by a strange sequence of Spirit-anointed men raised up by God. Then in 1 Samuel we read the story of how first Saul and then David are made king over Israel. It is not until 2 Samuel 5:6–10 that David conquers Jerusalem.

Jerusalem

Jerusalem became enormously significant for the assembly of the people of God. We find its meaning especially celebrated in some of the psalms. I shall take Psalm 122 to give us four of the most important meanings of Jerusalem.

> I rejoiced with those who said to me,
> "Let us go to the house of the LORD."
> Our feet are standing
> in your gates, O Jerusalem.
> Jerusalem is built like a city
> that is closely compacted together.
> That is where the tribes go up,
> the tribes of the LORD,
> to praise the name of the LORD
> according to the statute given to Israel.
> There the thrones for judgment stand,
> the thrones of the house of David.
> Pray for the peace of Jerusalem:
> "May those who love you be secure.
> May there be peace within your walls
> and security within your citadels."
> For the sake of my brothers and friends,
> I will say, "Peace be within you."
> For the sake of the house of the LORD our God,
> I will seek your prosperity.

Each of Psalms 120 to 134 is headed 'A Song of Ascents'. The psalms in this collection are to be sung going 'up' to Jerusalem, probably by pilgrims going up for the great Jewish festivals like Passover or Tabernacles. These were the times of 'sacred assembly' when 'all Israel' gathered in Jerusalem (Lev. 23:4). They were not going 'up' because Jerusalem is an especially high mountain. It isn't all that high. Although it is in a hilly region, even the Mount of Olives is higher, and one of this same collection of psalms speaks of the mountains surrounding Jerusalem (Ps. 125:2)! No, they spoke of going 'up' because Jerusalem was important. In a similar way, in England we sometimes speak about going 'up' to London, because London is our capital city. In Old Testament terms, you could start your journey on the top of Mount Everest, but if you were going to Jerusalem, you had to go 'up': it was the most important place on earth. We shall see why.

There seems to be something of a progression in the first three psalms of the collection. Psalm 120 sings of the misery of living in a broken world. 'Too long,' sings the psalmist, 'have I lived among those who hate peace' (v. 6). He longs for peace, and in Psalm 121 he begins his journey up to Jerusalem, the city of peace; the Hebrew *salem* comes from 'shalom' meaning 'peace' (rather like the Arabic *salaam*). Jerusalem was the place on earth where peace was to be found. This is why the psalmist rejoices at the start of Psalm 122 when his friends suggest going up to Jerusalem on pilgrimage. This psalm is about the place of peace that speaks of the remaking of a world at war.

In verses 1 to 5 he rejoices in four characteristics of Jerusalem: a 'house' (v. 1), a 'city' (v. 3), united 'tribes' (v. 4) and 'thrones' (v. 5). Each of these will unlock a truth about the meaning of Old Testament Jerusalem: they speak of access, security, unity and government. We shall consider them in turn.

A. Access: Jerusalem is where God lives on earth

The psalm is bracketed by references to 'the house of the LORD' (vv. 1,9); this means the Temple, where God (in Old Testament symbolism) lived on earth. We saw in Chapter 1 that when Adam and Eve were expelled from the Garden of Eden a rift occurred between heaven and earth. From that time on the harmony of the universe was disrupted. Heaven became God's space *as opposed to* our human space, and 'earth' became the space (the material space-time universe) where God no longer lived in a direct relational way. But heaven began very soon to reinvade earth, to create meeting points – places and ways in which some kind of access to heaven might be enjoyed by the believer on earth.[38] The various altars erected by Abraham, Isaac and Jacob were such meeting places, and especially the altar on Mount Moriah where Abraham sacrificed the substitute ram in place of Isaac on the site where, centuries later, Solomon built the Temple (Gen. 22:1–19; 2 Chr. 3:1). So was the place where Jacob had a dream of a ladder reaching from earth to heaven (Gen. 28:10–22). In the wilderness between Sinai and the Promised Land, the Tabernacle (or Tent) fulfilled this role (Exod. 25 – 40). In the Tabernacle was the special box (the Ark of the Covenant) containing the two stone tablets inscribed with the Ten Commandments; this was pictured as being the 'footstool' under God's throne, the place where God placed his feet on earth.[39] Finally, the mobile Tabernacle was replaced by Solomon's Temple (1 Kgs 5 – 8).

The Tabernacle and the Temple were designed to echo the Garden of Eden in a number of ways.[40] Just as God 'walked' in the garden, so he 'walks' among his people in the Tabernacle and Temple.[41] The garden was entered from the East and guarded by cherubim; in the same way the Tabernacle and Temple were entered from the East and guarded by cherubim.[42] Just as the garden is a source of a life-giving river, so Ezekiel's Temple vision has a life-giving river flowing out of the Temple (Gen. 2:10; Ezek. 47:1–12). The Tabernacle contained a branched lampstand (the Menorah) and the Temple had tree decorations on its pillars, both of which may symbolize the Tree of Life (Gen. 2:9; 3:22; Exod. 25:31–35). In these and other ways the Tabernacle and Temple were meant at least to hint that access might one day be possible back into the Garden of Eden.

The reason sinful people could come close to a holy God is this was the place of sacrifice. The utterly fair but steady and hot anger of God against sinners was poured out, in symbolic form, on an animal sacrifice, so that the sacrifice was burnt up in the place of the worshipper. The sacrifice was (in the technical term) a 'propitiation', which means a sacrifice which appeases wrath. In Chapter 6 we shall see this fulfilled at the Cross.

Verse 2 of the psalm is spoken in tones of awe and wonder. How wonderful, he sings, that now at last our feet can stand within the gates of Jerusalem itself! He is amazed to stand within the gates of the city where God lives. He knows he does not deserve it: no-one deserves it. He stands there by grace. He feels the wonder of the presence of God in the city of peace. This is the place that God loves. The same sense of wonder is evident in Psalm 87, with its vision that from all over the world people will see no higher privilege than to have been 'born' in Zion, a vivid way of speaking of their identity as children of Zion, and therefore children of God. We find a deep sense of longing to be in Zion also in Psalm 84, where the singers yearn and faint with longing, crying out to be in the presence of the living God: they can hardly wait until they, with other pilgrims, appear before God in Zion (vv. 1,2,7).

Having said all this, we must remember the access given to the immediate presence of God was still very limited. Just as at Sinai only Moses (or Moses with Aaron and the elders) could go onto the mountain, so in the Temple only the priests could go in, and only the High Priest into the Holy of Holies, and that only once a year and with great care. Nevertheless, there is a sense of wonder that God dwells among his people. The Tabernacle at the centre of the camp in the wilderness, and the Temple at the heart of Jerusalem, foreshadowed the day in the future of which Hebrews 12 speaks, when all the people of God have unconstrained access to God because of Jesus.

For our theme of scattering and gathering, here is a significant point to note: Israel are gathered in Jerusalem *around the presence of God* to show they can only be gathered to one another when they are *first gathered to God.*

B. Security: Jerusalem is the only truly safe place on earth

In Psalm 122:3 the psalmist looks round at Jerusalem and exclaims,

Jerusalem is built like a city that is closely compacted together.

Our translation makes it sound a bit like Singapore, as though 'closely compacted together' meant having a high housing density! He does not mean this at all. He means it is a solid city, with no fractures in its walls, no weaknesses in its defences, and not divided against itself. It is not like Berlin from the 1950s to the 1980s, with a dividing wall down the middle. He looks around and sees Jerusalem as a rock-solid secure place in an insecure world: it is impregnable. 'Look around,' he sings, 'at this safe place, this solid place, this city with foundations and walls, this place that cannot be attacked or shaken. This is a place of solidity, of glory, of weight, of substance, of great stone buildings and fine stone walls. I feel safe here inside these gates.'

A few years ago when I was visiting Japan there was a great scandal breaking out. Because Japan suffers frequent earthquakes, the cities have strict building regulations governing the earthquake-proofing of high-rise buildings. A prominent architect in Tokyo was arrested and charged with falsifying the earthquake-proofing certificates for a number of these buildings. If this was true, it was obviously very serious. Buildings that appeared secure were actually likely to fall down when the earthquake came. It is a picture of the false security offered by idols. A 'career ladder' invites us to get on the first rung and climb up and up and up, feeling safe inside that 'building': the reality is if we trust our careers for security, when the shocks of God's judgment storms come, we will find the earthquake-proofing we had been promised was a fraud.

But Jerusalem in Old Testament symbolism is the only really safe place on earth. This sense of security, that the people of God can safely assemble here, is apparent in other places. We see this confidence in Psalm 125, another of the Psalms of Ascent: 'Those who trust in the LORD are like Mount Zion, which cannot be shaken but endures for ever' (v. 1). Psalm 48 is a great celebration of 'Mount Zion, the city of the Great King' which is 'secure forever' even though it will be attacked (vv. 2,8).

Perhaps the most vivid Old Testament drama of the security of Jerusalem happened when the Assyrian King Sennacherib attacked and surrounded it during the reign of King Hezekiah. The people of God were assembled, even huddled, together within the besieged walls that must have seemed so fragile and vulnerable. But God wonderfully protected his city so they could even laugh with scorn at their attacker (2 Kgs 18 – 19; see especially 19:21). To assemble in the place where God lives is to gather in safety.

The hymn writer John Newton (the author of 'Amazing Grace') expressed this wonderfully in his great hymn:

> Glorious things of thee are spoken,
> Zion, city of our God.
> He, whose word cannot be broken,
> Form'd thee for his own abode:
> On the Rock of Ages founded,
> What can shake thy sure repose?
> With salvation's walls surrounded,
> Thou may'st smile at all thy foes.

C. Harmony: Jerusalem is the only place where warring tribes unite

The third thing about Jerusalem that makes the psalmist rejoice (and this lies close to the heart of our theme of gathering) is in verse 4. Jerusalem is the place where the usually quarrelling tribes of Israel unite in worship.

> That is where the tribes go up,
> the tribes of the LORD,
> to praise the name of the LORD
> according to the statute given to Israel.

Jerusalem is the only place where warring tribes can be brought together in peace. On the journey from Sinai to

Jerusalem, Israel was just as divided and fractious as the rest of the human race. This is particularly seen in the tensions between the tribes. Much of Joshua is taken up with allocating sections of the conquered land to the different tribes (Josh. 13 – 21). This includes some territory to the east of the Jordan, which had been conquered first and was allocated to the tribes of Reuben and Gad, and the half-tribe of Manasseh. We come very close to a civil war between these two and a half tribes and the rest in Joshua 22. Tribal tensions are never far below the surface in Judges. We see these tensions, for example, when the Ephraimites are angry with Gideon, who is from Manasseh, or when the Ephraimites (again!) are angry with Jephthah the Gileadite (Judg. 8:1; 6:15; 11:1; 12:1). Judges ends with the whole tribe of Benjamin being threatened with genocide by the other tribes (ch. 20, 21)! The history of Israel is a history of tribal conflict. We continue to see this later in Israel's history with the conflicts between Saul's followers in the tribe of Benjamin and David's from the tribe of Judah, and in the civil war that followed Solomon's death. The tribes of Israel are not naturally united: far from it. By nature they are as disunited as the original sons of Jacob from whom they were descended. They unite only when they agree to 'go up', and when they go up, they then bow down in worship, adoration and praise, not of themselves but of the God who has redeemed them. When they seek to 'climb up' to their own towers like Babel, they end up at war and scattered.

There are actually only two options for human society: true worship and war. Only true worship humbles human pride. False worship and war go together, because false worship exalts the worshipper, who is really only worshipping an idol of their creation or imagination. Only in worship of the true God will people be brought so low our aspirations to greatness will be removed, and our empire-building plans abandoned. Only in true worship will we live together in weakness and without pretensions.

The psalmist rejoices to see men and women from different tribes going up with him to Jerusalem to worship and praise God together. He loves to see fellow believers humbled together under the mighty hand of God to offer praise to the Redeemer God rather than seeking praise for themselves.

The theme of 'assembly' is one of the ways the psalms often speak of Jerusalem. 'Praise God in the great congregation; praise the LORD in the Assembly of Israel'.[43] Worship and praise are the key to successful gathering of naturally warring tribes. The psalmist feels the wonder of united thanksgiving in the city of peace.

D. Government: Jerusalem is the place from which God's king rules the world

The fourth reason the psalmist rejoices to be in Jerusalem is in Psalm 122:5. Jerusalem is the place from which God's anointed king rules.

> There the thrones for judgment stand,
> the thrones of the house of David.

One of the reasons Israelites went on pilgrimage to Jerusalem was to have their legal business attended to by the highest courts in the land. This was the place where the judges sat (hence the plural 'thrones'). We might speak of going to where the Supreme Court or the High Court sits. Those judges were just if – and only if – they served a just king.

The Old Testament equivalent of a coronation was an anointing. Instead of placing a crown on the king's head, you poured oil over him (see, e.g., the anointing of David in 1 Sam. 16:1–13). He became the 'anointed one', for which the Hebrew word is 'Messiah' and the Greek word 'Christ'. The psalmist is glad to go to Jerusalem because that is where God's anointed one, God's king, God's Messiah, God's Christ, rules with justice.

To understand why the psalmist is so glad, we need to go back in Israel's history to the time before they were ruled by God's anointed king. Without a strong king, a people will end up scattered.

One way of looking at gathering and scattering is in terms of whose side we are on in a war. It is common imagery to speak of a leader assembling troops for battle, and a defeated army being scattered.[44] Sometimes the Old Testament speaks of the LORD as a warrior leading his people to victory. They often spoke of God's enemies being scattered.[45] Of course, this is a double-edged truth. It means if my enemies are God's enemies, my enemies will be scattered: but it also means if I worship idols, then I will be among the scattered, for I will have lined myself up with God's enemies. I cannot have it both ways, living without God and expecting to stay gathered in peace.

To be saved is to be gathered together with the whole people of God under God's leader; I cannot be saved as an individual without being gathered to God's people. We see this clearly in the climax of a great prayer King David later gave to the people: '*Save* us, O God our Saviour; *gather* us and deliver us from the nations . . .'; to be saved is to be gathered out of the nations into the presence of God (1 Chr. 16:35).

This military use of the gathering and scattering imagery raises the question of the human leadership of the people of God. Who is going to be God's delegated instrument to gather the people for victory and stop them being scattered to the four winds?

They certainly needed such a leader. Tribal tensions and strife were particularly bad during the period of the 'Judges'. In many ways judges like Gideon, Samson and Jephthah seem more like local tribal warlords than leaders of all Israel. The writer of Judges leaves us in no doubt that the problem is that they have no overall God-given leader. The final chapters of Judges paint a terrible picture of social breakdown (Judg. 17 – 21). This is punctuated four times by a refrain which makes the cause clear:

> 'In those days Israel had no king; everyone did as he saw fit.' (17:6)
> 'In those days Israel had no king.' (18:1)
> 'In those days Israel had no king.' (19:1)
> 'In those days Israel had no king; everyone did as he saw fit.' (21:25)

The point is that scattering is not an unusual phenomenon in Israel: it is the default state of Israel, as it is the default state of every human society, following the pattern of Babel. If Israel is to be united, they must be given a king. So when we begin the books of Samuel the question in our minds is, 'Will Israel have a king, and if so, what sort of king?' That question is answered when, after a long story, David becomes king.[46] One of the very first things he did was to conquer Jerusalem, 'the fortress of Zion' which he renamed 'the city of David' (2 Sam. 5:6–9).

David was a shepherd or pastor. From the time of David onwards there was a particularly strong association between kingship and shepherding. A shepherd in those cultures was the leader and protector of his flock. Without his protection the flock will be scattered by wolves, 'harassed and helpless, like sheep without a shepherd', 'scattered because there was no shepherd' (Matt. 9:36; Ezek. 34:5). A shepherd gathers his flock together in safety (see, e.g., 2 Sam. 7:5–16).

Old Testament Jerusalem and the Jerusalem of Promise

So in verses 1 to 5 of Psalm 122, the psalmist looks around Jerusalem with the eyes of faith. He sees the place on earth which combines the presence of God, the security of the people of God, the harmonious gathering of the people of God and the just government of God's Christ. These four themes are closely connected. The reasons Jerusalem is so safe and peaceful are the presence of God and the rule of God's Christ. Because God is there in the Temple and rules his people by his king, Jerusalem is a place of harmony and security. Stable and lasting gathering is possible only in the presence of God under the government of God's king.

All this Jerusalem signifies, and all this our pilgrim sees with the eyes of faith. For the moment he looks around at the actual historical Jerusalem, he knows he will be sadly disappointed. Instead of being a place of security, all too often it was a place where the weak were oppressed. Instead of being a place of unity, all too often it was a place of massive social inequality. Instead of being a place where justice was done, all too often it was just the opposite. For example, in Isaiah's day, we read that God 'looked (in Jerusalem) for justice, but saw bloodshed; for righteousness, but heard cries of distress' (Isa. 5:7).

It is because the real Old Testament Jerusalem fell far short of the Jerusalem of promise that the psalmist ends with exhorting us to pray that the city called the 'city of peace' will live up to its name.

> Pray for the peace of Jerusalem:
> "May those who love you be secure.
> May there be peace within your walls
> security within your citadels."
> For the sake of my brothers and friends,
> will say, "Peace be within you."
> For the sake of the house of the LORD our God,
> I will seek your prosperity.

All through the disappointments of Israel's history the promise kept being repeated, that one day there would be a Jerusalem that really lived up to its name. Here is one of the most famous of those prophecies:

> This is what Isaiah son of Amoz saw concerning Judah and Jerusalem:
> In the last days
> the mountain of the LORD's temple will be established
> chief among the mountains;
> will be raised above the hills,
> all nations will stream to it.
> Many peoples will come and say,
> "Come, let us go up to the mountain of the LORD,
> to the house of the God of Jacob.
> He will teach us his ways,
> so that we may walk in his paths."
> The law will go out from Zion,
> the word of the LORD from Jerusalem.
> He will judge between the nations
> and will settle disputes for many peoples.

They will beat their swords into plowshares
and their spears into pruning hooks.
Nation will not take up sword against nation,
nor will they train for war any more. (Isa. 2:1–4 (substantially repeated in Mic. 4:1–3))

Here, in vision, is a city to which we must indeed go 'up', for it is now 'established as chief among the mountains . . . raised above the hills'. The whole world will gather there ('all nations will stream to it' – a wonderful picture of a fragmented world being reassembled in Jerusalem). They go there because this is the place from which God's instruction ('the law . . . the word of the LORD' v. 3) goes out from Zion. It is the place where just judgment will at last be done (v. 4), disputes settled, wars ended and harmony established on earth at last. This is the significance of Jerusalem in Bible language.

Where is Jerusalem today?

This will be a good point in our journey to pause and ask, 'Where is Jerusalem today?' That may seem a silly question, but it is not. We have seen Jerusalem in Bible language was not only a physical place but also meant something, and what it meant did not correspond with what it was actually like on the ground. When we read the language of Jerusalem in our Bibles today, what should we be thinking about? What does the writer of the letter to the Hebrews mean by saying to Christian people that when they assemble for church they, 'have come to Mount Zion, to the heavenly Jerusalem' (Heb. 12:22)?

Here are four pointers which will anticipate some themes we shall explore later in our Bible tour. The first is a necessary negative. The second, third and fourth are positive.

1. 'Jerusalem' is not in the Middle East

Under the Old Covenant, in Old Testament times, Jerusalem was quite simply and literally a place, a city. You could find it on a map. You can find where it *was*, in a Bible atlas. But Jerusalem in a Bible atlas, or Jerusalem the capital of the state of Israel, is not the same as Jerusalem in New Covenant Bible significance. When today under the New Covenant we speak of Jerusalem, we are not speaking of travelling to the Middle East. If we were, then Christianity would be an elite religion in which those who could afford the tours were more privileged than poor Christians who could not. But Christianity is the very opposite of an elite religion.

The reason Jerusalem now does not have the significance of Jerusalem then is very simple: what made Jerusalem significant then was the Temple, the place on earth where God dwelt. But in AD 70 the Temple was destroyed. Indeed the New Testament speaks sadly of the physical Jerusalem after Jesus: it even calls it the place of judgment, the place of spiritual slavery (Gal. 4:25).

All through Israel's history there was this tension between Jerusalem as spoken of in faith, and the historical reality. Gradually, they began to grasp that the physical Jerusalem, like everything else in the Old Covenant, was but a shadow pointing forward to a substantial reality to be revealed later.

2. 'Jerusalem' is fulfilled in the Lord Jesus Christ

Supremely Jerusalem meant what the Temple meant, the presence of God on earth, the one place on earth where human beings could meet God without being burnt alive.

But 2000 years ago one who is greater than the Temple stood on earth (Matt. 12:6). He 'made his dwelling among us' (literally 'tabernacled among us', fulfilling among us what the Tabernacle had meant in the wilderness) (John 1:14). Jesus spoke of his body as a 'Temple' that would be destroyed and then 'rebuilt' in three days (John 2:19–22). On the Cross he was the place where sinful human beings can meet with God without being destroyed: all that Jerusalem symbolized is fulfilled in Jesus. He is the place where we meet God, the place where we are secure, the place where squabbling people can unite, and the place where God's king rules on earth.

3. 'Jerusalem' is foreshadowed in the local church

What Jerusalem means is anticipated now on earth in the local church. Jesus is to be found now on earth where his people gather. They, corporately as local churches, are God's Temple, the place where God dwells among his people by his Spirit (1 Cor. 3:16). (The individual Christian's body is also called a 'temple of the Holy Spirit' as an incentive to sexual purity (1 Cor. 6:19), but the major emphasis is corporate rather than individual (e.g. 2 Cor. 6:16; Eph. 2:21,22).) They are being built into a spiritual house, a temple, and therefore, by the Spirit of God, the local church is a partial fulfilment of 'Jerusalem' (1 Pet. 2:5). It is a local expression and foretaste, an anticipation, a foreshadowing, a partial but real expression of 'Jerusalem' here on earth.

4. 'Jerusalem' is waiting to come down from heaven to fill the earth

Hebrews 12 speaks of coming to 'the heavenly Jerusalem' (v. 22). One day the real and final Jerusalem will come down from heaven to earth, and fill the earth, and be the New Creation (Rev. 21:2). We shall develop this theme in Chapter 9.

So 'Jerusalem' is focused on Jesus, anticipated and partially experienced in the local church, and will be fully and finally experienced in the New Creation.

What does 'Jerusalem' mean for local church life?

Each of the themes of Psalm 122 can be traced forward into the life of a local church. Just as the psalmist grieves and feels the pain of living in a broken world (Psalm 120), so we ought to be able to long for our local church meetings as God's supernatural antidote to a broken world. They ought to be places where the presence of God is known on earth by his Spirit, where real and lasting security is found in an insecure and dangerous world, where harmony is experienced by 'tribes' who would naturally be at war, and where a people commit themselves to being governed in justice by God's Christ through his word. A local church that expresses, albeit partially and imperfectly, something of what Jerusalem promised in the Old Testament, will be God's instrument for remaking a broken world. We shall explore these themes further in Chapter 8.

Questions for Discussion

1. In what ways have you experienced the 'woe is me' of living in a warlike world and being unable to make peace (Ps. 120:6)?
2. Review the teaching from Psalm 122. What major features of Jerusalem did we note?
3. Have you experienced in the context of Christian fellowship,

(a) the joy of knowing we have access together to God in Jesus?

(b) the assurance of knowing that in Jesus we are secure for ever?

(c) the surprise and wonder of finding people who would not usually get along together actually beginning to love one another?

(d) a shared agreement to submit to Jesus Christ as God's king ruling his people by his word the Bible?

4. What should we expect in a local church? How do we cope when our experience is disappointing? How should this sharpen our hope for the New Creation?

5

Babylon: Back to Babel

And then it all fell apart. The gathering at Sinai and the regular assemblies in Jerusalem all ended in terrible scatterings. This chapter is themed all around 'Babylon', but by 'Babylon' I mean the theological idea of 'Babylon' and not just the historical city of Babylon. Babylon is a paradoxical 'place' in the Bible, as it is the place to which the people of God are scattered. How can you be scattered to a place?! Of course on the map it was a city (now in Iraq), the capital of the Neo-Babylonian empire, and later a significant city in the Persian empire. But in Bible language 'Babylon' is a 'place' standing for many places, or no fixed place: it is a place defined by where it is not (i.e. Jerusalem) rather than by where it is. To 'go to Babylon' is not to assemble in Babylon, but to be scattered to Babylon. It is a place only in the sense that outer space is a place.

From Jerusalem to Babylon

We now move in overview over a vast sweep of Old Testament history, all the way from the great united kingdom of all Israel under King David and his son

King Solomon, to the final scattering in the Babylonian exile in 587 BC. We are going to greatly simplify this sweep of history and look at three significant 'scattering events', in each of which the unity of the people of God was broken.

A. The tearing apart of the kingdom into Israel and Judah

The first fracture happened almost immediately after King Solomon's death. The seeds of division had been sown during Solomon's reign as he imposed slave labour on the Israelites and so broke the law of God. Solomon was not faithful to the LORD and the result, as always, was strife (1 Kgs 5:13–16; 11:1–43). One particular source of trouble was a capable civil servant called Jeroboam, who had a meeting with a prophet called Ahijah. This is what happened:

> About that time Jeroboam was going out of Jerusalem, and Ahijah the prophet of Shiloh met him on the way, wearing a new cloak. The two of them were alone out in the country, and Ahijah took hold of the new cloak he was wearing and tore it into twelve pieces. Then he said to Jeroboam, "Take ten pieces for yourself, for this is what the LORD, the God of Israel, says: 'See, I am going to tear the kingdom out of Solomon's hand and give you ten tribes. But for the sake of my servant David and the city of Jerusalem, which I have chosen out of all the tribes of Israel, he will have one tribe. I will do this because they have forsaken me and worshiped Ashtoreth the goddess of the Sidonians, Chemosh the god of the Moabites, and Molech the god of the Ammonites, and have not walked in my ways, nor done what is right in my eyes, nor kept my statutes and laws as David, Solomon's father, did.

> "'But I will not take the whole kingdom out of Solomon's hand; I have made him ruler all the days of his life for the sake of David my servant, whom I chose and who observed my commands and statutes. I will take the kingdom from his son's hands and give you ten tribes. I will give one tribe to his son so that David my servant may always have a lamp before me in Jerusalem, the city where I chose to put my Name."' (1 Kgs 11:29–36)

Jeroboam's new cloak was dramatically torn into twelve pieces, as a sign that the unity of Israel was going to be torn apart after Solomon's death. Ten tribes would follow Jeroboam and the remaining two (Judah and Benjamin, sometimes spoken of as just one, because Benjamin was so small) would remain in David's dynasty. This happened at the start of the reign of Solomon's son Rehoboam (1 Kgs 12).

Israel now became the name, no longer of the whole people of God, but just of the ten tribes in the northern kingdom, with its capital at Samaria. The rest, just two tribes, were named after the bigger of the two, Judah (from which we get our word 'Jew'), and continued with kings in David's line and his capital Jerusalem. This terrible event is described as God tearing Israel away from the house of David (2 Kgs 17:21). From that day onwards the tribes never went unitedly up to Jerusalem to worship. Solomon's unfaithfulness to God led to scattering of the people of God. Harmony is only possible in faithful fellowship with God.

B. The scattering of the northern kingdom by Assyria

The second scattering event was when the northern kingdom was itself scattered by Assyria. Jeroboam became the first king of an independent Israel. He had been promised by the prophet Ahijah if he was faithful to the LORD, he too could found an enduring dynasty. He proved himself the exact opposite of faithful to the LORD, setting up a rival religion.[47] 1 Kings 12 to 2 Kings 17 tells the two interlinking stories of Israel and Judah. The story of the northern kingdom came to an end in the year 729 BC when the inhabitants were deported to various different places by the king of Assyria (2 Kgs 17:1–6). The territory of the ten northern tribes was resettled by the king of Assyria with a random mixture of peoples, who settled down to an eclectic pick'n'mix of religions; their descendants were the religiously-mixed and despised people later called the Samaritans (as in the parable of the Good Samaritan) (17:7–41).

The prophet Hosea spoke to the northern kingdom shortly before this happened. In a terrible acted parable of Israel's unfaithfulness he marries Gomer, an unfaithful wife, and she bears a daughter and a son by other men. Hosea is to call the girl 'Lo-Ruhamah', which is the Hebrew for 'unloved'; he is to call the boy 'Lo-Ammi', the Hebrew for 'not-my-people' (Hos. 1:1–9). At the very heart of the disaster that befalls Israel is the fracture in their covenant relationship with the LORD: this is why they are scattered.

C. The scattering of Judah to Babylon

The final and climactic scattering was the exile of the southern kingdom Judah to Babylon. Judah survived precariously for a little over a century after the northern kingdom had been wiped off the map until in 587 BC the Neo-Babylonian empire, which had succeeded the Assyrian empire as regional superpower, invaded Judah and finally sacked Jerusalem, destroying Solomon's magnificent Temple and taking the people into exile (2 Kgs 18 – 25). It makes terrible reading.

D. The scattering of the covenant curse

So by these three traumatic scatterings God's wonderful gathering was effectively destroyed. All the hopes that a broken world would be remade through Abraham's family seemed to be dashed. God had promised a remade world: but the paradox was it was the God who made the promise who did the scattering. Again and again the Bible says that although these scatterings happened through the processes of politics and international affairs, behind these forces lay the determined and deliberate will of God acting in just judgment (the human powers that 'scattered Judah, Israel, and Jerusalem' are called 'horns' in Zech. 1:19).

Right at the start of Israel's life, when God first made a Covenant with them, he made it clear if they were unfaithful to him they would be scattered. Moses said this to them repeatedly:

> 'if you . . . become corrupt and make any kind of idol, doing evil in the eyes of the LORD and provoking him to anger, . . . The LORD will *scatter* you among the peoples'; 'if you do not obey the LORD your God . . . The LORD will cause you to be defeated before your enemies. You will come at them from one direction [i.e. as a gathered army] but flee from them in seven [i.e. as a scattered rabble]'; 'Then the LORD will *scatter* you among all nations, from one end of the earth to the other'. (Deut. 4:25–27; 28:15,25,64)

Idolatry separates people from the one God who alone can enable them to live in harmony. A community that will not bow before the God who is One is bound to end up scattered, just as the builders of Babel were dispersed.

Retelling the story of the LORD's faithfulness and Israel's unfaithfulness, Psalm 106 recounts that,

Then they despised the pleasant land [i.e. the Promised
Land];
they did not believe his promise.
They grumbled in their tents
and did not obey the LORD.
So he swore to them with uplifted hand
that he would make them fall in the desert,
make their descendants fall among the nations
and *scatter* them throughout the lands. (vv. 24–27)

Psalm 44 laments that in the exile,

You gave us up to be devoured like sheep
and have *scattered* us among the nations. (v. 11)

Towards the end of Judah's existence, the prophet
Jeremiah made himself very unpopular by some forceful
preaching of the covenant curses. He often used the language of scattering.

The LORD said, 'It is because they have forsaken my law . . .
Therefore . . . I will *scatter* them among nations that neither
they nor their fathers have known . . .' (9:13–16)

The shepherds [that is, the leaders of Israel, who ought to have
been doing what David was anointed to do] are senseless
and do not enquire of the LORD;
so they do not prosper
and all their flock is *scattered*. (10:21)

I will scatter you like chaff
driven by the desert wind. (13:24)

Like a wind from the east,
I will *scatter* them before their enemies;

I will show them my back and not my face
in the day of their disaster. (18:17)

Notice how alienátion from God – 'I will show them my
back . . .' – leads to being scattered before their enemies.

'Woe to the shepherds who are destroying and *scattering* the
sheep of my pasture!' declares the LORD . . . '. . . you have
scattered my flock and driven them away and have not
bestowed care on them . . .' (23:1,2)

And so, when it happened, Jeremiah could lament:

The LORD himself has *scattered* them;
he no longer watches over them. (Lam. 4:16)

Ezekiel says something very similar:

Also with uplifted hand I swore to them in the desert that I
would *disperse* them among the nations and *scatter* them
throughout the countries, because they had not obeyed my
laws . . .[48]

Looking back many years later, the prophet Zechariah
can say God was the primary agent who caused this scattering:

'When I called, they did not listen; so when they called, I
would not listen,' says the LORD Almighty. 'I *scattered* them
with a whirlwind among all the nations, where they were
strangers'. (7:13,14)

Again and again the prophets and the psalms said
God would do it: and when it had happened, they said
God had done it. Apart from loyal fellowship with God,

human community will always be unstable and the 'Tower of Babel' principle will come into play bringing scattering. This is precisely what happened to the Old Testament people of God.

The Significance of Babylon

What does Babylon mean in the Bible? In terms of our scattering/gathering tour, I want to focus on three characteristics of Babylon.

A. *Babylon is the opposite of Jerusalem*

The most obvious thing about Babylon is it was not Jerusalem. Everything Jerusalem symbolized, Babylon was not. Perhaps the most famous psalm lamenting the exile is Psalm 137. This is a psalm about two cities: Babylon experienced and Zion remembered. Jerusalem is remembered, but the tragedy is it cannot be experienced, and therefore its songs cannot be sung.

> By the rivers of Babylon we sat and wept
> when we remembered Zion.
> There on the poplars
> hung our harps,
> for there our captors asked us for songs,
> tormentors demanded songs of joy;
> they said, "Sing us one of the songs of Zion!"
> How can we sing the songs of the LORD
> in a foreign land?
> If I forget you, O Jerusalem,
> may my right hand forget its skill.
> May my tongue cling to the roof of my mouth
> I do not remember you,

if I do not consider Jerusalem
my highest joy.

The last part of the psalm (vv. 7–9) expresses in anguished terms the pain of the exiles at being torn away from Jerusalem. The believers amongst them treasured Jerusalem as the place where the people of God gathered in harmony and security in the presence of God under the government of God's Christ.[49] Babylon was the opposite of all of these, a place of scattering rather than harmony, danger rather than security, separation from God and the absence of God's Christ. It is defined by what it is not: there is no vision informing Babylon, no reality, no substance, no life.

B. Babylon is the place of human pride

Isaiah 13:1 – 14:23 contains a sustained judgment on Babylon. It emphasizes especially the sheer selfish pride of the place. It seems to symbolize the proud sin of the world in general.

I will punish the world for its evil,
the wicked for their sins.
I will put an end to the arrogance of the haughty
and will humble the pride of the ruthless. (13:11)

Because it is so proud of its power and achievements, it rides roughshod over others and is a place of oppression and aggression (14:4–6). In a strong echo of the builders of the Tower of Babel (Gen. 11:4), God says,

You said in your heart,
'I will ascend to heaven;
I will raise my throne
above the stars of God;

I will sit enthroned on the mount of assembly,
on the utmost heights of the sacred mountain [i.e. the
mountain of God]. (Isa. 14:13)

In Isaiah 47, Babylon expresses her proud heart when
she says, 'I am, and there is none besides me'; I exist for
me, and no-one else exists except insofar as they do
things for me (v. 8). No-one else matters. The pride of
Babylon makes it a selfish place, and therefore a divided place, a place where people treat other people
brutally. This was the agonizing memory of Psalm
137:8,9, remembering the heart-rending cruelty of the
Babylonians. Babylon is the very opposite of the city of
peace.

C. Babylon is like hell on earth

Although it is, geographically, a location, relationally it is
a scattering, a place where there may be physical proximity to people but there is relational alienation, a place
where deeply scattered people happen to be living close
together. The poet Shelley said that, 'Hell is a city much
like London': the same could be said of anywhere where
community is based on the pride and principles of
Babylon. There will be proximity without intimacy,
crowdedness without relationship and locality without
community.

A terrible and vivid appropriation of the hellish
metaphor of Babylon is Kenneth Anger's cult book
Hollywood Babylon.[50] Anger tells how the 'Star system'
was born in the 1910s, but how in the midst of the drug-
induced euphoria and sexual chaos there was an ever-
present fear, 'that the bottom could drop out of their
gilded dreams at any time'. He called Hollywood 'the
Wonder World of Make Believe', a dream factory (pp.

7,15,17). But it was all so ephemeral and it destroyed so many lives, as Anger catalogues with horrifying detail. Hollywood, like Babylon, was a place of lies, promising pleasure and providing misery.

A friend of mine tells of a bumper sticker that read, 'Paratroopers don't die; they just regroup in hell.' But they don't: no-one 'regroups' in hell. Hell is a place of separation, a far cry from the popular idea of a raucous and pleasure-filled party.

C.S. Lewis conveys the sheer loneliness of scattering, in his imaginative novel about Hell, *The Great Divorce*. His narrator is given a bus tour of a vast grey town which seems to go on and on forever but to have hardly anyone living in it. He asks his neighbour on the bus why this is:

> The trouble is that they're so quarrelsome. As soon as any-one arrives he settles in some street. Before he's been there twenty-four hours he quarrels with his neighbour. Before the week is over he's quarrelled so badly that he decides to move. Very likely he finds the next street empty because all the people there have quarrelled with *their* neighbours – and moved. If so he settles in. If by any chance the street is full, he goes further. But even if he stays, it makes no odds. He's sure to have another quarrel pretty soon, and then he'll move on again . . .[51]

Although Babylon promises all the fun of a raucous pub or a wild orgiastic party, it ends up with a desperate scat-tered loneliness. In the lonely terrors of hell there is no gathering, no friendship, no love, no loyalty and no affection, nothing to soften the sheer misery of having nothing and no-one beyond my selfish self to relate to. This is what Babylon means.

After Babylon

In the five or so centuries after Babylon, the people of God had to live with two realities in tension. On the one hand, there was a partial and, to be honest, very disappointing 'end' to the exile; and yet on the other they carried with them a growing chorus of prophetic voices which insisted God had not given up on his promise to remake the world through Abraham's descendant. Let us consider these in turn.

A. A partial regathering after the exile

In about 539 BC Cyrus absorbed the neo-Babylonian empire into what later became the vast Persian empire. His policy was to send subject peoples back to their homelands and indeed to encourage them to build temples and worship the gods and goddesses of those lands. The Jews were included in this policy (2 Chr. 36:22,23) and, under the leadership of the scribe Ezra and the political governor Nehemiah, and inspired by the vigorous prophetic preaching of Haggai and Zechariah, several groups of them returned to Jerusalem to rebuild the Temple and the city walls, and to begin again the life of the people of God in what became the province of Judah in the Persian Empire.

Nehemiah sees this political development as the fulfilment of God's promise to gather his scattered people. Before he returns to Jerusalem from the Persian capital Susa, Nehemiah prays and reminds the LORD of his promise

> "Remember the instruction you gave your servant Moses, saying, 'If you are unfaithful, I will *scatter* you among the nations, but if you return to me and obey my commands, then even if your exiled people are at the farthest horizon, I

will *gather* them from there and bring them to the place I have chosen as a dwelling for my Name'". (1:8,9)

This programme of resettlement and rebuilding had its setbacks and its encouragements over a number of years, and amongst the encouragements were some very positive gatherings or assemblies.[52] There was one particularly wonderful assembly which must have reminded those with good biblical memories of the foundational assembly at Sinai and the joyful assemblies in Jerusalem before the exile. It is recorded in Nehemiah 8.

When the seventh month came and the Israelites had settled in their towns, all the people assembled as one man in the square before the Water Gate. They told Ezra the scribe to bring out the Book of the Law of Moses, which the LORD had commanded for Israel.

So on the first day of the seventh month Ezra the priest brought the Law before the assembly, which was made up of men and women and all who were able to understand. He read it aloud from daybreak till noon as he faced the square before the Water Gate in the presence of the men, women and others who could understand. And all the people listened attentively to the Book of the Law.

Ezra the scribe stood on a high wooden platform built for the occasion. Beside him on his right stood Mattithiah, Shema, Anaiah, Uriah, Hilkiah and Maaseiah; and on his left were Pedaiah, Mishael, Malkijah, Hashum, Hashbaddanah, Zechariah and Meshullam.

Ezra opened the book. All the people could see him because he was standing above them; and as he opened it, the people all stood up. Ezra praised the LORD, the great God; and all the people lifted their hands and responded, "Amen! Amen!" Then they bowed down and worshiped the LORD with their faces to the ground.

The Levites – Jeshua, Bani, Sherebiah, Jamin, Akkub, Shabbethai, Hodiah, Maaseiah, Kelita, Azariah, Jozabad, Hanan and Pelaiah – instructed the people in the Law while the people were standing there. They read from the Book of the Law of God, making it clear and giving the meaning so that the people could understand what was being read. (vv. 1–8)

They assemble as all Israel to hear and obey the word of God. It must have been a wonderful encouragement to taste this joyful assembling of the people of God in Jerusalem again, as the people of God gather in harmony 'as one man' (v. 1) under the word of God, the pattern of Sinai being worked out again in the life of Israel.

But was the exile really over? If we remember how Psalm 122 celebrated the house of the LORD, the security of the city, the unity of the tribes and the just rule of the king in David's line, then we may see there was a very partial re-establishment of the first two but nothing at all to bring back the third and fourth (See pp. 73–78). There was a new Temple, although a very much smaller and poorer one than Solomon's wonderful building. The prophet Haggai asks the Second Temple builders, 'Who of you is left who saw this house in its former glory [i.e. Solomon's Temple]? How does it look to you now? Does it not seem to you like nothing?' (Hag. 2:3). The city walls were rebuilt which must have just begun to give a fragile sense of security. But the unity of the tribes was never re-established, since the ten 'lost tribes' from the former northern kingdom never came back, and indeed the majority of the southern tribes never chose to return from exile. Later, in the time of Esther, the Jews were described as 'a certain people *dispersed and scattered* among the peoples in all the provinces' of the Persian empire (Esth. 3:8). They formed a great Diaspora (which means 'Dispersion' or 'Scattering') to the east, south, west and north of the Promised Land. Every time these Diaspora Jews sang Psalm 106 they cried to the LORD,

> Save us, O LORD our God,
> and *gather* us from the nations,
> that we may give thanks to your holy name
> and glory in your praise. (v. 47)

Above all, there was no king, even though Zerubbabel was a descendant of David and some must have hoped he might become king. However, he remained a 'governor of Judah', firmly under the thumb of the Persian empire (Hag. 1:1; Matt. 1:12).

B. A chorus of prophecies of a reassembled world

So the promises of a gathered people in fellowship with God, ruled by God's king, and through whom a broken world would be regathered, remained very sadly unfulfilled. And yet – paradoxically – alongside the sad reality of continued scattering, there remained a chorus of voices from all periods of Israel's history, crying out God was going to gather them together at last under Abraham's descendant. Here is a sample of these voices, to help us appreciate just how often the promises for the future were expressed in terms of the gathering of a scattered people. There are more examples that could be chosen.

From the prophet Isaiah:

> 'he will . . . *gather* the exiles of Israel; he will *assemble* the
> scattered people of Judah . . .'; '*gathered* up one by one'; 'he
> tends his flock like a shepherd; he *gathers* the lambs in his
> arms' (notice the link between gathering and shepherding);
> 'I will bring your children from the east and *gather* you from
> the west'; 'to bring Jacob back to him and *gather* Israel to
> himself' (notice the link between gathering to God and
> gathering back to one another); 'with deep compassion I
> will *gather* you'; 'he who *gathers* the exiles of Israel; I will
> *gather* still others to them, besides those already *gathered*';
> 'all *assemble* and come to you; your sons come from afar'; 'I
> am about to *gather* all nations and tongues, and they will
> come and see my glory.'[53]

From the prophet Jeremiah:

> 'I myself will *gather* the remnant of my flock'; 'I will *gather*
> you from all the nations'; '*gather* them from the ends of the
> earth'; 'He who *scattered* Israel will *gather* them and will
> watch over his flock like a shepherd'; 'I will surely *gather*
> them from all the lands'[54]

From the prophet Ezekiel:

> 'Although I sent them far away among the nations and *scat-*
> *tered* them among the countries, yet . . . I will *gather* you
> from the nations and bring you back from the countries
> where you have been *scattered*'; 'When I *gather* the people of
> Israel from the nations where they have been *scattered*'; 'As
> a shepherd looks after his *scattered* flock when he is with
> them, so will I look after my sheep. I will rescue them from
> all the places where they were *scattered* on a day of clouds
> and darkness. I will bring them out of the nations and

gather them from the countries'; 'I *dispersed* them among the nations, and they were *scattered* through the countries . . . I will *gather* you from all the countries and bring you back'; 'I will take the Israelites out of the nations where they have gone. I will *gather* them from all around and bring them back into their own land . . . There will be *one king* over all of them and they will *never again be two nations or be divided into two kingdoms*'; 'when I have brought them back from the nations . . . though I sent them into exile . . . I will *gather* them'[55]

From the prophet Hosea:

'Yet the Israelites will be like the sand on the seashore, which cannot be counted [echoing the promise to Abraham]. In the place where it was said to them, "You are not my people", they will be called "sons of the living God". The people of Judah and the people of Israel will be *reunited* [reversing the tearing apart of the kingdom], and they will appoint *one leader* and will come up out of the land [that is, the land of exile] . . .' (1:10,11; see also 2:14–23)

From the prophet Micah:

'I will surely *gather* all of you, O Jacob; I will surely bring together the remnant of Israel. I will *bring them together* like sheep in a pen, like a flock in its pasture'; '"In that day," declares the Lord, "I will *gather* the lame; I will *assemble* the exiles and those I have brought to grief."' (2:12; 4:6)

From the prophet Zephaniah:

'From beyond the rivers of Cush my worshippers, my *scattered* people, will bring me offerings. . . . At that time I will deal with all who oppressed you; I will rescue the lame and *gather* those who have been *scattered*. I will give them praise and honour in every land where they were put to shame. At that time I will *gather* you; at that time I will bring you home.' (3:10,19,20)

From the prophet Zechariah:

'I will signal for them and *gather* them in. Surely I will redeem them; they will be as numerous as before. Though I *scatter* them among the peoples, yet in distant lands they will remember me.' (10:8,9)

All these prophecies insist God is going to do a great gathering, even though it was painfully obvious even by the very end of the Old Testament period he had not done it yet.

Conclusion

Again and again, these voices from God reaffirmed the promise to Abraham, that in his descendant the whole world would be blessed and there would be a great gathering. The scattering of Israel's Old Testament history would one day be reversed. What do we learn from putting these voices alongside the Old Testament realities of Israel's life? The reality was that Israel was, for the most part, indistinguishable from the rest of the world east of Eden, scattered from the Tower of Babel. Their wonderful history ended, more or less, in Babylon, right back at Babel again.

We learn from this the assemblies patterned for us at Sinai and then Jerusalem were foreshadowings of the gatherings God would do to fulfil his promise to Abraham, but were not the gatherings themselves. They were realistic practice exercises to show us what the real gatherings would be like. These assemblies were, as it were, scale models of the real thing. Although all through Israel's history there were some real believers, by and large Old Testament Israel did not exhibit the evidence of being the true people of God. So these assemblies are in the Bible to show us the pattern for the real gatherings, which are the assemblies of the local Christian church. These churches, the realization (that is to say, the 'making real') of the promise of God, did not become possible until two great New Testament events had taken place, the Cross of Christ and the outpouring of the Holy Spirit at Pentecost. These great events are the subjects for the next two chapters.

Questions for Discussion

1. Review the survey in this chapter of what happened from Jerusalem to Babylon. What were the main stages in the disintegration of the people of God? What caused this?
2. Have you seen the pride of Babylon in our society, in leaders and in your own heart? How does it express itself?
3. Have you experienced 'places' like Babylon, places of relational scattering in which people are alienated from one another?
4. How do these experiences serve to warn us of the lonely terrors of hell?
5. Review what happened after the exile in Babylon. In what ways was it disappointing, and in what ways encouraging?
6. How can the life of a local church answer in practice the longings of lonely people?

Section C

The Assembly of Jesus: Gathering Realized

6

Golgotha: Gathered to Jesus

Our Bible tour takes us now to the centre of human history and the place where all the gatherings and scatterings of the Old Testament begin to make sense, 'Golgotha, the place of the Skull' where they crucified Jesus (Mark 15:22). The Bible story so far is full of puzzles. One big puzzle is this: on the one hand we have a broken world, excluded from Eden, shattered and living in the long shadow of the Tower of Babel. This is the consequence of human pride and rebellion against God. On the other hand, we have the promise of God who has said he will reunite the world through Abraham's descendant, and seemed to begin to do that through the assembly at Sinai and then the joyful gatherings at Zion. And yet now our story is (spiritually) scattered in Babylon; we might as well be back at the Tower of Babel. So how is the God who promised to reunite the world going to keep his promise?

The Earthly Ministry of Jesus

Expectations of gathering

What would a believing Jew have been thinking around the year zero, between what we now call BC and AD? We meet one such believer in Luke 2:25–35. His name is Simeon and he is one of my favourite minor characters in the Bible; I think he should be nominated for a Bible Oscar for 'Best Supporting Actor'. When Simeon is introduced, Jesus was very young, and Joseph and Mary were taking him to the Temple for a Jewish ceremony.

Luke introduces him like this: 'Now there was a man in Jerusalem called Simeon, who was righteous and devout.' This didn't just mean he kept the Law of Moses outwardly: it also meant in his heart he loved God and believed the promises God had made to Abraham. Because he believed the promises, Luke goes on, 'He was waiting for the consolation of Israel . . .' Simeon would have been painfully aware of living in a broken world, and could no doubt have sung Psalm 120 with feeling (see p. 68). He knew God had promised to remake the broken world through Abraham's descendant. He remembered the amazing assembly at Mount Sinai (how could any pious Jew forget!) and he treasured all Jerusalem symbolized in the promises of God. But he knew it had all ended in tears and scattering, finally to Babylon. And in his heart he seems to have known this scattering had never really ended. There was still no sign of an assembly of nations, the real United Nations, through Abraham's descendant (Gen. 28:3; 35:11; 48:4). Most deeply, he felt the pain of Israel there was not yet the promised king in David's line, the Messiah or Christ. How could the world be remade until God's Christ came? Only this descendant of Abraham could be 'the consolation of Israel', the one who fulfils the promises to Abraham, and remakes a broken world.

Wonderfully, God had revealed to Simeon he would not die before he had seen God's Messiah. It must have been very surprising for Joseph and Mary as they took the baby Jesus into the Temple and were met by this man, who took the baby in his arms and began to pray,

> Sovereign Lord, as you have promised,
> you now dismiss your servant in peace.
> For my eyes have seen your salvation,
> which you have prepared in the sight of all people,
> a light for revelation to the Gentiles
> and for glory to your people Israel. (Luke 2:29–32)

Simeon understood this child was God's Christ who would bring a rescue to finally remake a broken world. Mary herself had sung a Spirit-inspired song during her pregnancy, in which she had celebrated that God

> has scattered those who are proud
> in their inmost thoughts
> . . . but has lifted up the humble
> . . . has helped his servant Israel,
> remembering to be merciful
> to Abraham and his descendants for ever,
> even as he said to our fathers. (Luke 1:51–55)

Mary knew about the scattering of Babel, the scattering of the proud, and she had just begun to understand her baby would be the one through whom God kept his promises to Abraham. So maybe when she thought about it, Simeon's song won't have come as such a surprise.

Matthew too drops a big hint Jesus came to gather. He begins his gospel with a carefully structured genealogy of Jesus.

> A record of the genealogy of *Jesus Christ* the son of *David*, the son of *Abraham*:
>
>> *Abraham* was the father of . . . King *David*,
>> *David* was the father of . . . and Josiah the father of Jeconiah and his brothers at the time of *the exile to Babylon.*
>> After *the exile to Babylon*: . . . and Jacob the father of Joseph, the husband of Mary, of whom was born *Jesus, who is called Christ.*
>
> Thus there were fourteen generations in all from *Abraham* to *David*, fourteen from *David* to *the exile to Babylon*, and fourteen from *the exile* to *the Christ*. (1:1–17)

By artificially missing out some of the generations, Matthew structures his genealogy to make the point there are three critical people or events to bear in mind when thinking about the Christ (Messiah). These are (a) Abraham (who was promised his offspring would inherit the world), (b) David (who was promised he would rule the world from Zion), and (c) the exile to Babylon. So Jesus Christ will be: (a) 'the son of Abraham', i.e. the descendant of Abraham who will inherit the world; (b) 'the son of David' who will rule the world in justice from 'Zion'; and (c) at last the one who brings the scattering of exile to an end. Jesus is the Christ who will gather a broken world together again under the rule of the one God.

The apostle Paul wrote, 'no matter how many promises God has made, they are "Yes" in Christ' (2 Cor. 1:20).

Given so many of these promises are couched in the language of a great gathering, we shall not be surprised to find Jesus Christ is the key to this gathering.

The earthly ministry of Jesus who gathers his church

When Jesus of Nazareth was about thirty years old, a massive religious movement swept Judea. At the centre of it was a strange man called John the Baptist, a powerful preacher of repentance. John made it clear his was just a preparatory movement to get ready for Jesus, who was much greater than himself. One of the ways he described this much greater man was in terms of a farmer at harvest:

> His winnowing fork is in his hand, and he will clear his threshing floor, *gathering* his wheat into the barn and burning up the chaff with unquenchable fire. (Matt. 3:12)

Gathering is what Jesus does. From the moment he started his public ministry, Jesus began to gather. Right at the start he called disciples to follow him, and said they too would become gatherers, fishers of people.

> As Jesus was walking beside the Sea of Galilee, he saw two brothers, Simon called Peter and his brother Andrew. They were casting a net into the lake, for they were fishermen. "Come, follow me," Jesus said, "and *I will make you fishers of men*." At once they left their nets and followed him.

> Going on from there, he saw two other brothers, James son of Zebedee and his brother John. They were in a boat with their father Zebedee, preparing their nets. Jesus called them, and immediately they left the boat and their father and followed him. (Matt. 4:18–22)

Jesus gathers; and those he gathers, begin to gather with him. Crowds flocked to him (see e.g., Matt. 4:23–5:1). Jesus was a magnet. He reached out especially to outsiders and unlikely people. To the leper, by definition excluded both from God's presence in the Temple and from the people of God, Jesus reached out his hand: he touched him, made him well and brought him in (8:1–4). He ate in fellowship with the despised tax-collectors and notorious 'sinners', calling one of them to be an apostle; he was known as the friend of sinners (9:9–11; 11:19). It was a characteristic mark of his ministry that 'tax collectors and "sinners" were all gathering round to hear him' (Luke 15:1). He declares one chief tax-collector is 'a son of Abraham', bringing him in to Abraham's people (19:9). We saw in Chapter 1 death is the cruellest and most painful form of separation or scattering. So it is not surprising to find in Jesus' earthly ministry he gathers people from death itself. He meets a mother grieving her dead son who has been separated from her by death, restores the young man to life and gives him back to his mother; mother and son become, as we might say, a reassembled family (7:11–17)!

In an echo of Old Testament shepherd passages (especially Ezekiel 34) Jesus looks at the crowds and longs to gather them in, as a farmer gathers a harvest into a barn or a shepherd his sheep into a sheepfold.

> Jesus went through all the towns and villages, teaching in their synagogues, preaching the good news of the kingdom and healing every disease and sickness. When he saw the crowds, he had compassion on them, because they were harassed and helpless, like sheep without a shepherd. Then he said to his disciples, "The harvest is plentiful but the workers are few. Ask the Lord of the harvest,

therefore, to send out workers into his harvest field."
(Matt. 9:35–38)

He tells his disciples he is determined to build his
'church', his assembly (16:18). The Old Testament
Assembly of Israel pointed forward to the Assembly of
Jesus. One day he will return to this earth to 'gather his
elect from the four winds, from one end of the heavens
to the other' (24:31).

In an important 'gathering' section of John's gospel
(John 9 and 10), Jesus first reaches an outsider, a man
born blind, a man who most people thought was tainted
in some dangerous way by sin (9:1,2). Jesus brings this
man in, and is vigorously opposed by the Pharisees, who
would have been happy to keep him outside. Jesus follows up this controversy by speaking of himself as the
Good Shepherd, again picking up Old Testament 'shepherd' passages. Jesus is the only truly good leader for the
people of God: and he is also the one who will at last
gather them from all over the world.

> I am the good shepherd; I know my sheep and my sheep
> know me – just as the Father knows me and I know the
> Father – and I lay down my life for the sheep. I have other
> sheep that are not of this sheep pen. I must bring them also.
> They too will listen to my voice, and there shall be *one flock
> and one shepherd*. (10:14–16)

It is vital to Jesus' ministry both that he gathers, and that
those he gathers become gatherers of all sorts of other
people. Indeed, 'he who does not gather with me scatters' (Matt. 12:30). There is no neutral position: Jesus is
like a magnet who magnetizes the iron filings attracted
to himself. Gathering is vital and central to what Jesus
does.

And yet Jesus also divides

And yet, although gathering is what Jesus does and is the activity close to his heart, he warns his gathering will also divide, because not all will submit to be gathered to him.

> Do not suppose that I have come to bring peace to the earth. I did not come to bring peace, but a sword. For I have come to turn
> 'a man against his father,
> a daughter against her mother,
> a daughter-in-law against her mother-in-law –
> a man's enemies will be the members of his own household.'
> Anyone who loves his father or mother more than me is not worthy of me; anyone who loves his son or daughter more than me is not worthy of me; and anyone who does not take his cross and follow me is not worthy of me. Whoever finds his life will lose it, and whoever loses his life for my sake will find it.' (Matt. 10:34–39; see also Luke 12:49–53)

In the parable of the wedding banquet Jesus speaks of the kingdom of heaven as a feast from which those first invited excuse themselves, but at which all sorts of unlikely people find themselves gathered and seated in the end (Matt. 22:1–14; Luke 14:15–24).

Shortly before the end of his earthly life, he laments the refusal of so many in Jerusalem to let him gather them in.

> O Jerusalem, Jerusalem, you who kill the prophets and stone those sent to you, how often I have longed to gather your children together, as a hen gathers her chicks under her wings, but you were not willing. (Matt. 23:37)

The only people who were excluded from his welcome were those who were sure they didn't need it and despised those who knew they did need it.

> As Jesus went on from there, he saw a man named Matthew sitting at the tax collector's booth. "Follow me," he told him, and Matthew got up and followed him.
>
> While Jesus was having dinner at Matthew's house, many tax collectors and "sinners" came and ate with him and his disciples. When the Pharisees saw this, they asked his disciples, "Why does your teacher eat with tax collectors and 'sinners'?"
>
> On hearing this, Jesus said, "It is not the healthy who need a doctor, but the sick. But go and learn what this means: 'I desire mercy, not sacrifice.' For I have not come to call the righteous, but sinners." (9:9–13)

Jesus gathers: but some will be left outside. He gathers all kinds of people without distinction of race, culture, class, or moral respectability. But he does not gather all people without exception. Some despise his gathering grace. He came as a doctor for the sick; the only people excluded from his welcome are those who insist they are not sick (and thereby show they are deluded).

Commending the faith of a Gentile Roman centurion, he said in the great gathering at the end of time there would be some surprising people included (those who trusted him) and some horrified people excluded (horrified, because they thought they deserved to be insiders). There will be a terrible 'outside', a place of eternal exile, a scattering with no return.

> I say to you that many will come from the east and the west, and will take their places at the feast with Abraham, Isaac

and Jacob in the kingdom of heaven. But the subjects of the kingdom will be thrown outside, into the darkness, where there will be weeping and gnashing of teeth. (Matt. 8:11,12)

So the earthly ministry of Jesus shows us both gathering and exclusion. All sorts of unlikely men and women are gathered into Jesus' church, his assembly; and yet all sorts of surprised people, who thought they ought to be insiders, find themselves outside of Jesus' church. We shall understand this only at the Cross, because it is only by the scandalous death of Jesus he can gather his church, and it is those who are offended by the Cross who exclude themselves from his church.

Gathered at Golgotha: Only at the Cross of Jesus is a Broken World Remade

During Jesus' earthly ministry his apostles saw all sorts of things they did not fully understand at the time. When the gospels were written later, they sometimes put in explanatory comments to show what the events and teaching of Jesus' life meant. Matthew includes one of these comments in the middle of an account of Jesus' healing ministry.

When evening came, many who were demon-possessed were brought to [Jesus], and he drove out the spirits with a word and healed all the sick.
This was to fulfil what was spoken through the prophet Isaiah:
"He took up our infirmities
and carried our diseases." (Matt. 8:16,17)

Matthew quotes from one of the famous songs in Isaiah about a future 'Servant of the LORD', which means someone who is in faithful covenant relationship with the Lord. The song Matthew quotes from is Isaiah 52:13 to 53:12 and includes the prophecy this Servant will suffer and die to pay the punishment for the sins of the people. I doubt if Matthew understood this at the time, but later when he wrote his gospel he saw Jesus could only heal and gather during his earthly ministry because he was going to die to pay the penalty for sinners.

As Jesus' earthly ministry continued, those with him saw all manner of wonderful examples of gathering as Jesus healed, forgave, and brought men and women into his new community, his church. But as time drew on there was a mounting sense of foreboding: for Jesus said again and again he was going to be killed (Mark 8:31; 9:31; 10:33,34).

When the Jewish leaders were plotting to kill Jesus, Caiaphas the high priest said something more profound than he realized:

> Then one of them, named Caiaphas, who was high priest that year, spoke up, "You know nothing at all! You do not realise that it is better for you that one man die for the people than that the whole nation perish." (John 11:49–50)

What Caiaphas meant was a simple truth of realpolitik: it would be better for this tiresome imposter and troublemaker to be killed, than to allow him to start a rebellion the Romans would surely crush and so destroy the whole nation. But John goes on to explain there was something deeper going on than even Caiaphas the speaker realized:

> He did not say this on his own, but as high priest that year he prophesied that Jesus would die for the Jewish nation,

and not only for that nation but also for the scattered children of God, to bring them together and make them one. (11:51–52)

Caiaphas spoke more truly than he realized: he prophesied, that is, he said what God wanted said. The full God-given meaning of what he said is an extraordinarily vivid echo of our theme of scattering and gathering. Jesus will die in order 'to bring together' 'the scattered children of God' 'and make them one': that is, he will die finally to bring to an end all that the exile symbolized, that terrible scattering we saw at the Tower of Babel, and the exclusion from the garden of Eden. All the scattering of a broken world will be healed and gathered at the Cross of Jesus Christ.

Jesus himself understood this. As he anticipates the cross, he says, 'I, when I am lifted up from the earth' (that is, lifted up on the cross) 'will draw all men' (that is, all kinds of people without distinction) 'to myself' (John 12:32). Jesus does not promise to draw or gather all human beings without exception to himself. Elsewhere he has made it clear some will be excluded (e.g. Matt. 8:10–12). He means that on the cross he will draw to himself all kinds of people without distinction of race, gender, moral respectability, privilege, culture or talents. In particular, he will gather to himself, into his church, people who failed to fulfil the Law of Moses.

The Law of Moses was the great divider of humanity in the culture and land of Jesus: either you were in or you were out. The great guardians of the law were the Pharisees, who were quite sure they were in and most other people were out. The surprise was the people who thought they were in were actually out, and all sorts of people who were regarded as being out were drawn in by Jesus. Jesus was very rude about the people who were sure they were 'righteous' and called them 'white-washed tombs', with the outward appearance of being clean but actually being very dirty inside (Matt. 23:27). These are the people who think of themselves as being members of the kingdom of God, but who will end up 'thrown outside, into the darkness, where there will be weeping and gnashing of teeth' (8:12). This must prompt us to ask how anyone can get inside, be gathered into the people of God.

We need to think back in our Bible journey to the covenant curses of scattering. We saw at the Tower of Babel God scatters the proud. He always has, he always does, and he always will. When he made a covenant with his people, he called them to depend on him in humble trust, to believe his promises to Abraham and to live as faithful and obedient people. If they don't, then again and again God warns them they will be scattered: this is exactly what happened (see pp. 85–88). The law of God given at Sinai is a very good law. If people lived like that then humanity would be wonderfully united and harmoniously gathered. There would be no need for policemen, for locks, for aid agencies; there would be no hunger, no poverty, no war and no cruelty. But we don't and we won't live like this because our hearts are the same as the hearts of the builders of the Tower of Babel. We live under the curse of the law, and it is entirely our fault.

What happened at the Cross of Jesus is that God took upon himself in the person of his Son the curse of the law. There is an Old Testament law that says a man who is 'hung on a tree' (public execution and disgrace) is 'under God's curse' (Deut. 21:22,23). His public execution is a sign he is guilty and rightly condemned by God. When Jesus died on a wooden cross, the early Christians understood his public disgrace meant exactly this: he was under the curse of God. So Paul writes,

Christ redeemed us from the curse of the law by becoming a curse for us, for it is written: "Cursed is everyone who is hung on a tree." (Gal. 3:13)

God made him who had no sin to be sin for us (2 Cor. 5:21)

All the right and fair hot anger of God against sinners was poured out on God at the Cross of Jesus. He became 'sin'; he became 'a curse'; and he did it 'for us'. Books have been written, will be written, and ought to go on being written, on the wonderful truth of the Cross.[56] But for the purposes of our thematic study, I want us to notice only this sin-bearing death, this death that takes on itself the wrath of God, is able to reconcile human beings to God – and therefore make it possible for human beings to be reconciled to one another.

The reason the Cross is the focus of worldwide gathering is only at the Cross does God make peace between God and sinful people. Only at the Cross are we given peace and reconciliation with God (Rom. 5:1,10,11). And therefore only at the Cross can we be reconciled to our fellow human beings.

Jesus came as the doctor to those who know they need healing. Those who are happy as they are, confident in their own ability to live in proud autonomy, exclude themselves from his healing and gathering work. The Cross is both the focus of worldwide gathering and at the same time the great divider. It is offensive to human pride to be told I can contribute nothing to my right standing with God, and to be told I cannot build stable lasting human society without Jesus dying to pay the penalty for my sin. I would much prefer to think I can do it on my own. Only those who are humbled by the Cross can live together in love and harmony, because only those men and women have nothing to prove and nothing to hide.

In Chapter 8 we shall explore much more fully what the Cross means for the local church, and how the local church can only experience real God-given unity at the foot of the Cross.

The President of the United States is sometimes called, 'The leader of the free world'. It is a fine title and there have been times when the world has had cause to be very grateful to America and some American presidents. But ultimately there is only one man who is qualified to bear this title. He bears it because he alone has done what was necessary to bring a broken and enslaved world into freedom, peace and unity. It is because the Cross is so utterly crucial (literally) to the remaking of a broken world only Jesus can be the leader of that new world. One day the world will bow the knee to the one who died. This is why he alone can be entrusted with 'All authority in heaven and on earth' (Matt. 28:18). This is why Paul can call people from all over the world to bow the knee in 'the obedience of faith' in Jesus (Phil. 2:6–11; Rom. 1:5; 16:26).

Questions for Discussion

1. Review what we have seen of the earthly ministry of Jesus. How have we seen him acting as a magnet to draw people together? Can you think of other examples from the gospels?
2. What kinds of people kept their distance from Jesus, and why?
3. Why is the Cross the only way to draw all kinds of people together?
4. Why do some people find this offensive?
5. Have you seen the local church becoming a magnet for all kinds of needy people, as Jesus was?

6. If not, what is stopping this happening? How can we help outsiders understand we are not superior to them, but invite them to join us at the foot of the Cross?

7

Pentecost: Gathered by the Spirit

In our tour of the Bible, we have made some long jour-
neys between our main stops. From Sinai to Jerusalem
took hundreds of years: so did Jerusalem to Babylon,
and Babylon to Golgotha. Our next journey takes just a
few weeks: but what amazing weeks! We move now
from that earth-changing day at the Cross to a day just a
few weeks later, also in Jerusalem, at the Jewish festival
of Pentecost. Before we get there, however, we need to
wind back the clock to some prophecies given in exile in
Babylon.

The Promise of the Spirit to Gather the People of God

We have seen Israel was given a chorus of prophecies
that one day God would remake his broken world (see
pp. 99–102). We are going to focus now on the prophecies in Ezekiel 34 to 37: we shall see these prophecies
connect the gathering of Israel with the outpouring of
the Spirit of God.

Ezekiel 34 is a sustained judgment on the selfish and
unfaithful leaders (shepherds) of Israel. As a result of

their evil leadership God's 'sheep' have been 'scattered' and 'became food for all the wild animals'; 'My sheep wandered over all the mountains and on every high hill. They were scattered over the whole earth, and no-one searched or looked for them' (vv. 5,6). Because the shepherds are not doing their job, God promises he will do it himself: 'As a shepherd looks after his scattered flock when he is with them, so will I look after my sheep. I will rescue them from all the places where they were scattered on a day of clouds and darkness. I will bring them out of the nations and gather them from the countries, and I will bring them into their own land' (vv. 12,13). He will do this by placing over them 'one shepherd, my servant David, and he will tend them' (v. 23).

Ezekiel 36:24–38 comes back to this theme of gathering: 'For I will take you out of the nations; I will gather you from all the countries and bring you back into your own land.' But this time the focus is on the people themselves, and their need for cleansing and forgiveness: 'I will sprinkle clean water on you, and you will be clean; I will cleanse you from all your impurities and from all your idols. I will give you a new heart and put a new spirit in you; I will remove from you your heart of stone and give you a heart of flesh. And I will put my Spirit in you and move you to follow my decrees and be careful to keep my laws' (vv. 24–27). Only a people whose hearts are changed can live in the land securely and harmoniously gathered, because only this people will live in harmony with God's peace-giving way of life (his law). This change of heart can only come about by a spiritual heart transplant, which is the work of the Spirit of God himself.

This prophecy is immediately followed by the famous prophecy of the valley of dry bones in Ezekiel 37:1–14.

The hand of the LORD was upon me, and he brought me out by the Spirit of the LORD and set me in the middle of a valley; it was full of bones. He led me back and forth among them, and I saw a great many bones on the floor of the valley, bones that were very dry. He asked me, "Son of man, can these bones live?"

I said, "O Sovereign LORD, you alone know."

Then he said to me, "Prophesy to these bones and say to them, 'Dry bones, hear the word of the LORD! This is what the Sovereign LORD says to these bones: I will make breath enter you, and you will come to life. I will attach tendons to you and make flesh come upon you and cover you with skin; I will put breath in you, and you will come to life. Then you will know that I am the LORD.'"

So I prophesied as I was commanded. And as I was prophesying, there was a noise, a rattling sound, and the bones came together, bone to bone. I looked, and tendons and flesh appeared on them and skin covered them, but there was no breath in them.

Then he said to me, "Prophesy to the breath; prophesy, son of man, and say to it, 'This is what the Sovereign LORD says: Come from the four winds, O breath, and breathe into these slain, that they may live.'" So I prophesied as he commanded me, and breath entered them; they came to life and stood up on their feet – a vast army.

Then he said to me: "Son of man, these bones are the whole house of Israel. They say, 'Our bones are dried up and our hope is gone; we are cut off.' Therefore prophesy and say to them: 'This is what the Sovereign LORD says: O my people, I am going to open your graves and bring you up from them; I will bring you back to the land of Israel. Then you, my people, will know that I am the LORD, when I open your graves and bring you up from them. I will put my Spirit in you and you will live, and I will settle you in your own land. Then you will know that I the LORD have spoken, and I have done it, declares the LORD.'"

The dry bones are a picture of a scattered Israel under judgment. This is clear from verse 11: 'these bones are the whole house of Israel. They say, "Our bones are dried up and our hope is gone; we are cut off."' In the vision, Israel is reconnected with itself in every way, gathered together to become 'a vast army' whom God will 'bring back to the land of Israel'. It is a picture of a supernatural gathering that will follow the scattering of exile. The climax of the vision is in verse 14: 'I will put my Spirit in you and you will live'. The 'breath' Ezekiel breathed in the vision is the same word as 'spirit', and pictures the breath or Spirit of God put inside the people of God to change them and give them life on the inside.

Immediately after this, in Ezekiel 37:15–28 we have a wonderful prophecy of a reunited north and south in Israel. Ezekiel is to take two sticks of wood, write the name of the southern kingdom on one and the northern kingdom on the other. Then he is to 'Join them together into one stick so that they will become one in your hand' (vv. 15–17). When asked to explain this prophetic visual aid, he is to say, 'This is what the Sovereign LORD says: I will take the Israelites out of the nations where they have gone. I will gather them from all around and bring them back into their own land. I will make them one nation in the land, on the mountains of Israel. There will be one king over all of them and they will never again be two nations and divided into two kingdoms . . . My servant David will be king over them, and they will have one shepherd' (vv. 21,22,24).

Putting these prophecies together we see the gathering of Israel, which is itself the beginning of the reversal of the scattering of Babel, will only happen when the Spirit of God is poured into the hearts of the whole people of God. Gathering cannot happen without the Spirit.

The Spirit and the Cross

The gift of the Spirit to the people of God will usher in the age of reconnection. But why the Cross? Why did Jesus need to die? Why could God not just decide it was time to pour out his Spirit on his people and gather them again? We can begin to understand the reason from John's gospel. In John 1:29–34, John the Baptist first says, 'Look, the Lamb of God, who takes away the sin of the world!' and only then says, 'The man on whom you see the Spirit come down and remain is he who will baptise with the Holy Spirit' (vv. 29,33). To 'baptise with the Holy Spirit' means to pour the Spirit of God into a human being so the person of God himself dwells inside him or her for ever. This is what happens when a man or woman becomes a real Christian. But only Jesus can give this gift. John the Baptist is filled with wonder Jesus will have the power to pour the very presence and person of God himself into a human heart: he knows no other religious leader, teacher or preacher can do this. He himself can baptize with water, giving the outward sign, but he cannot change a human heart (Matt. 3:11). And yet it becomes clear the only reason Jesus has this power is because he is the Lamb of God who dies on the Cross to take away sin.

Although the Spirit of God has been active ever since Creation, he could not be poured into human hearts in this lasting and permanent way until Jesus had died. In John 7, on the last day of the feast of Tabernacles, Jesus spoke about streams of living water flowing and bringing life. John explains, 'By this [Jesus] meant the Spirit, whom those who believed in him were later to receive. Up to that time the Spirit had not been given, since Jesus had not yet been glorified'; that is, glorified by being lifted up on the Cross (7:39).

The reason the Spirit could not be given until Jesus had died for sinners on the Cross is that if God came into an uncleansed human heart, he would destroy us. Because he is the Spirit of God, he is the Spirit of utter all-consuming holiness, the Holy Spirit: and holiness will destroy us unless our sin is cleansed by the Cross. To have the Spirit of the Holy God invading uncleansed human hearts would be like the people of Israel at Sinai wandering onto the mountain: it would have been more than their lives were worth. It is no light thing to have him in our hearts. This is why Jesus had first to die and only then could the Spirit be poured out to live in human hearts forever.

In the previous chapter we looked at Galatians 3:13, where Paul speaks of Jesus 'becoming a curse for us' (see pp. 119,120). In the next verse he tells us why Jesus did this:

> Christ redeemed us from the curse of the law by becoming a curse for us, for it is written: "Cursed is everyone who is hung on a tree." He redeemed us *in order that* the blessing given to Abraham might come to the Gentiles through Christ Jesus, so that by faith we might receive the promise of the Spirit. (3:13,14)

Jesus died so 'the blessing given to Abraham' (that is, the gospel promise that his offspring would inherit the world (Rom. 4:13) might spread right round the world ('come to the Gentiles'), so that anyone who comes to Jesus in faith would 'receive the promise of the Spirit.' The promise of the Spirit is central to the fulfilment of the promise to Abraham. The promise to Abraham can only be fulfilled when Jesus bears the curse and the Spirit is poured out on all who believe. Only the gift of the Spirit can enable the regathering of a broken world.

Pentecost: the Reversal of Babel

So after Jesus has died, and been raised from the dead as the proof his death has been effective, we are not surprised he tells his disciples to wait for the outpouring of the Spirit:

> Do not leave Jerusalem, but wait for the gift my Father promised, which you have heard me speak about. For John [John the Baptist] baptised with water, but in a few days you will be baptised with the Holy Spirit. (Acts 1:4,5)

They waited. While they waited, they appointed Matthias to replace Judas Iscariot and bring the number of the apostles back up to the symbolic number Twelve, a sign they were heads of a reconstituted or regathered Israel (1:12–26).

And then,

> When the day of Pentecost came, they were all together in one place. Suddenly a sound like the blowing of a violent wind came from heaven and filled the whole house where they were sitting. They saw what seemed to be tongues of fire that separated and came to rest on each of them. All of

them were filled with the Holy Spirit and began to speak in other tongues as the Spirit enabled them.

Now there were staying in Jerusalem God-fearing Jews from every nation under heaven. When they heard this sound, a crowd came together in bewilderment, because each one heard them speaking in his own language. Utterly amazed, they asked: "Are not all these men who are speaking Galileans? Then how is it that each of us hears them in his own native language? Parthians, Medes and Elamites; residents of Mesopotamia, Judea and Cappadocia, Pontus and Asia, Phrygia and Pamphylia, Egypt and the parts of Libya near Cyrene; visitors from Rome (both Jews and converts to Judaism); Cretans and Arabs—we hear them declaring the wonders of God in our own tongues!" Amazed and perplexed, they asked one another, "What does this mean?" (2:1–12)

They 'were all together in one place' (v. 1), as an assembly or gathering. But staying in Jerusalem at the same time were 'God-fearing Jews from every nation under heaven' (v. 5). Most of those could not have understood the little assembly of disciples if they had tried; they lived in the long shadow of the Tower of Babel. Ever since the Tower of Babel, the confusion of human languages, and the difficulties human beings have communicating properly, have been a terrible sign of living in the world outside Eden, the world under God's righteous curse on human pride.

Now, wonderfully and very surprisingly, the confusion of languages is briefly and miraculously overcome. Babel is reversed. At Babel the people sang their own praises, and so became incomprehensible to one another: at Pentecost, they sang the praises of the one God, and so began to understand one another. It is still now a wonderful thing to hear Christian brothers and sisters sing the praises of God, even when we cannot understand them. I remember on my first Sunday visiting a church in Japan listening as they sang a hymn in Japanese. Unlike the day of Pentecost, I didn't understand a word: but I had tears in my eyes as it came home to me one day we would understand one another perfectly, singing the praises of God and the Lamb for ever around the throne. The first Christian Pentecost anticipated that great day.

When the people ask Peter, 'What does this mean?' (v. 12), Peter preaches his famous Pentecost sermon, proclaiming to them the death, resurrection, ascension and glorification of Jesus as Lord and Messiah. When they ask, 'What shall we do?' (v. 37) he says,

> Repent and be baptised, every one of you, in the name of Jesus Christ for the forgiveness of your sins. And you will receive the gift of the Holy Spirit. The promise is for you and your children and for all who are far off – for all whom the Lord our God will call. (Acts 2:38,39)

The twin promises of forgiveness and the gift of the Spirit are given not only to Peter's hearers (mainly Jewish with a few proselytes), but also 'for all who are far off – for all whom the Lord our God will call.' This gospel gift, the Spirit of God given to every forgiven man and woman, will regather the scattered people of God and bring them together as one at last. He will remake a broken world.

This theme of a gathering spreading all over the world develops as the story of Acts is told. For example, in one of Peter's speeches he says his hearers are, 'heirs of the prophets and of the covenant God made with your fathers. He said to Abraham, "Through your offspring all peoples on earth will be blessed."' (Acts 3:25). The promise spreads to Samaria, that messed-up region that

testified to the miserable scattering of the northern kingdom by Assyria in 729 BC (see pp. 87,88); and then the
regathering spreads right out to the Gentiles (from Acts
10 onwards). This is God by his Spirit beginning the
work of remaking a broken world.

The Spirit of Unity

The reason the Spirit brings men and women together is
that he is the Spirit of the God who is One (see pp.
xii–xvii). By bringing men and women into fellowship
with God, he brings them into harmony with one another.
You and I cannot re-enter Eden without finding ourselves
side by side with one another. In London there are some
squares surrounded by houses, with a communal garden
in the middle, shared by all the residents. Eden is more
like this than individual little gardens in which each of
us can enjoy fellowship with God on our own! There is
one garden, where the God who is One walks with his
people.

In 1 Corinthians Paul writes to a church riven with
selfish divisions and overexcited about the gifts given by
the risen Christ to his people by his Spirit, wanting to use
those gifts to puff themselves up. To this divided church
Paul writes about the oneness of God:

> There are different kinds of gifts, but the same Spirit. There
> are different kinds of service, but the same Lord. There are
> different kinds of working, but the same God works all of
> them in all men. (1 Cor. 12:4–6)

Paul's point is there is one true God, Father, Son and
Holy Spirit. There are not three gods, but one God in
three persons. So when the Spirit of God really works in

human hearts, he brings them together. He is 'not a God of disorder but of peace' (14:33). The only reason Christians can ever manage to get along together in harmony is we have been given the Spirit of the God who is One.

Paul uses similar arguments in Ephesians 4:

> Make every effort to keep the unity of the Spirit through the bond of peace. There is one body and one Spirit – just as you were called to one hope when you were called – one Lord, one faith, one baptism; one God and Father of all, who is over all and through all and in all. (vv. 3–6)

The reason the various gifts are given is,

> so that the body of Christ may be built up until we all reach unity in the faith and in the knowledge of the Son of God and become mature. (vv. 12,13)

Gathered into the Fellowship of the Trinity

The deepest sense in which the Spirit of God gathers the people of God is he draws us into the fellowship of the Trinity. In thinking about this we are on holy ground. In the prologue to John's gospel, John tells us Jesus gives those who receive him the right to become children of God, to be gathered into the family of God:

> [the Word] came to that which was his own, but his own did not receive him. Yet to all who received him, to those who believed in his name, he gave the right to become children of God – children born not of natural descent, nor of human decision or a husband's will, but born of God. (1:11–13)

We are gathered into the family of God by a supernatural birth ('born of God'). We begin to understand how this supernatural birth can happen when Jesus speaks with the Jewish leader Nicodemus one night:

> Now there was a man of the Pharisees named Nicodemus, a member of the Jewish ruling council. He came to Jesus at night and said, "Rabbi, we know you are a teacher who has come from God. For no one could perform the miraculous signs you are doing if God were not with him."
>
> In reply Jesus declared, "I tell you the truth, no one can see the kingdom of God unless he is born again."
> "How can a man be born when he is old?" Nicodemus asked. "Surely he cannot enter a second time into his mother's womb to be born!"
>
> Jesus answered, "I tell you the truth, no one can enter the kingdom of God unless he is born of water and the Spirit. Flesh gives birth to flesh, but the Spirit gives birth to spirit. You should not be surprised at my saying, 'You must be born again.' The wind blows wherever it pleases. You hear its sound, but you cannot tell where it comes from or where it is going. So it is with everyone born of the Spirit." (John 3:1–8)

To be 'born again' (or 'born from above') means to be 'born of the Spirit'. The Holy Spirit gives supernatural new birth and makes a man or woman a child of God; he gathers them into fellowship with God. This truth of being gathered into fellowship with God is wonderfully developed by Jesus as he speaks to his inner circle of apostles in John 14 to 16.

> "If you love me, you will obey what I command. And I will ask the Father, and he will give you another Counsellor to

be with you forever – the Spirit of truth. The world cannot accept him, because it neither sees him nor knows him. But you know him, for he lives with you and will be in you. I will not leave you as orphans; I will come to you. Before long, the world will not see me anymore, but you will see me. Because I live, you also will live. On that day you will realise that I am in my Father, and you are in me, and I am in you. Whoever has my commands and obeys them, he is the one who loves me. He who loves me will be loved by my Father, and I too will love him and show myself to him."

Then Judas (not Judas Iscariot) said, "But, Lord, why do you intend to show yourself to us and not to the world?"

Jesus replied, "If anyone loves me, he will obey my teaching. My Father will love him, and we will come to him and make our home with him." (14:15–23)

When Jesus has died, risen, and ascended to the Father, he will ask the Father, and the Father will give to the disciples 'another Counsellor', that is, another who will be to them what Jesus has been to them while he was on earth. Jesus has brought them into fellowship with himself, and through him, into fellowship with the Father.

The promised other Counsellor will do the same. What is more, unlike Jesus who was taken from them, this Counsellor will be doing his work in them, 'for ever' (v. 16): he is already 'with' them in some sense, but from that future day onwards (the day of Pentecost) he will be 'in' them (v. 17). As he comes to them, Jesus himself will come back to them (v. 18), and give them his eternal life (v. 19).

Then, wonderfully, they will grasp what has happened (v. 20): just as Jesus is 'in' the Father (walking with him in unbroken fellowship and love), so they are 'in'

Jesus and he 'in' them. That is to say, the Counsellor has drawn them in to the fellowship of eternal love of the Trinity. In answer to the question (v. 22) as to what is special about all this (that is, what is unique here to the disciples that is not experienced by the world outside), Jesus replies: 'If anyone loves me, he will obey my teaching. My Father will love him, and we [Father and Son] will come to him and make our home with him' (v. 23). The Father and the Son come by the Spirit to make the home of God with the believer. The believer is drawn into the eternal fellowship of the Trinity.

Jesus returns to this theme in his great prayer of John 17. After praying for himself (vv. 1–5) and his apostles (vv. 6–19), his prayer broadens out as he prays for those who will believe in him through the testimony of the apostles.

> My prayer is not for them [the apostles] alone. I pray also for those who will believe in me through their message, that all of them may be one, Father, just as you are in me and I am in you. May they also be in us so that the world may believe that you have sent me. I have given them the glory that you gave me, that they may be one as we are one: I in them and you in me. May they be brought to complete unity to let the world know that you sent me and have loved them even as you have loved me. (vv. 20–23)

The 'oneness' and 'unity' God gives believers by his Spirit is the ultimate gathering and the end to all scatterings. There is no gathering more secure or more long-lasting than the eternal fellowship of the Trinity, and believers are brought in to this circle of everlasting love. In a very deep sense, this is Eden restored.

Questions for Discussion

1. Review the first section of this chapter. Why can the people of God not be reassembled until the Spirit of God is breathed into them?

2. Why can the Spirit not be given to live within people until after the Cross?

3. How did the day of Pentecost signal the scattering of Babel was going to be reversed? How did this reversal begin to happen after that day?

4. What experience do you have of the Spirit of God bringing a spiritual unity between Christians?

8

Church: Gathered Worldwide

God is Remaking the World through the Local Church

What do we think about, as we assemble with our local church, perhaps for a regular Sunday meeting? My guess is we mostly don't say to ourselves, 'This rather mixed and motley gathering of strange men and women (I include myself!) contains within it the cure for a broken world.' The thesis of this chapter, indeed the theme of the book, is precisely this: the ordinary local church with all its imperfections, weaknesses, oddities and problems, has within it the seeds, the spiritual and relational genetic blueprint, of a broken world remade. Here at last is not just God restraining human strife, but God actively gathering. There is in the church not just a treatment delaying the onset of scattering, but a cure actively replacing scattering with gathering.

It does seem hard to believe, but I want to persuade us it is true. When once we are fully persuaded of this, our attitude to our local church will never be quite the same again. So let me stress again: this chapter is not about some theoretical or idealized local church; it is about the local church as it actually is, all over the world.

There have been some helpful books written about the local church.[57] I am not going to try to duplicate these books, but rather to focus on how the local church fits in to our Bible overview, how it is in the present God's actual realized remaking of a broken world. All over the world we will see God rebuilding, repairing, remaking; and we see it in local churches.

We shall also have to address some obvious and forceful objections: religion is a divisive rather than uniting force in society; Christian churches are endlessly splitting rather than harmonious; and it is an observable fact on the ground that some local churches do the exact opposite of contributing to remaking a broken world. And yet I hope we shall end with a thoughtful and clear conviction the thesis is true.

The Local Church is a 'Scattered Gathering'

We begin with a paradox. So far we have seen a consistent theme through the Bible: the judgment of God leads to scattering and he shows his grace and faithfulness by gathering. Adam and Eve were 'scattered' from Eden in judgment for disobedience; the people at Babel were scattered as punishment for pride; Israel were gathered by God at Sinai and then again at Jerusalem, but scattered to Babylon in judgment. The cross is the place of gathering, and Pentecost is the gathering reversing the scattering of Babel.

Yet we are now to see a scattering that turns out to be the outworking of God's grace rather than God's judgment. This paradox is anticipated at the Cross. When Jesus was arrested, the disciples 'deserted him and fled' (Mark 14:50). Jesus knew this would happen and had told them it would be the fulfilment of a prophecy in Zechariah:

> "This very night you will all fall away on account of me, for
> it is written:
> 'I will strike the shepherd,
> and the sheep of the flock will be *scattered*.'" (Matt. 26:31)

He had warned them 'a time is coming, and has come, when you will be *scattered*, each to his own home' (John 16:32). This scattering seemed to contradict Jesus' statement on the Cross he would draw all kinds of people to himself (12:32): the exact opposite is the first thing that happened! And yet this terrible event, when the Shepherd who was promised to bring God's people together was killed and his followers scattered, turns out to be the key to a remade world.

The paradox continues after Pentecost: there is a great scattering that is the outworking of the faithfulness and rescue promises of God to gather a broken world. The days and weeks following Pentecost were filled with hostility to the church, culminating in the stoning of Stephen as the first martyr in Acts 7. Then we read,

> And Saul was there, giving approval to his death.
> On that day a great persecution broke out against the
> church at Jerusalem, and all except the apostles were *scattered* throughout Judea and Samaria. (Acts 8:1)

This was not the scattering of God's enemies, but of God's friends. But let us see what happened, as we read ahead in Acts.

> Now those who had been scattered by the persecution in
> connection with Stephen traveled as far as Phoenicia,
> Cyprus and Antioch, telling the message only to Jews. Some
> of them, however, men from Cyprus and Cyrene, went to

Antioch and began to speak to Greeks also, telling them the
good news about the Lord Jesus. The Lord's hand was with
them, and a great number of people believed and turned to
the Lord. (11:19–21)

As a result of the scattering of persecution, all sorts of
unlikely and distant people were gathered in to belong
to the Lord! Local churches began to be planted all over
the world. Those local churches are not 'scatterings' of
people under judgment: they are 'scattered gatherings',
by which people all over the world will be gathered in to
Jesus. They are scattered in order to reach the world; and
they are gathered locally as signposts to the final gathering of God's people at the end of time.

The Greek word translated 'church' (*ecclesia*) means
a congregation or assembly of people gathered together. It is the usual Greek word used to translate
the Hebrew word for the 'assembly' of Israel, from 'the
day of the assembly' at Mount Sinai onwards. The
'assembly' of Israel is a kind of prototype 'church'
(Acts 7:38, AV, 'the church in the wilderness'). A local
church is also called a 'synagogue', which also means
a gathering and is, of course, also used of the assemblies of Jewish people all over the Diaspora (Jas 2:2, NIV
'meeting'). Similarly, Paul uses the 'synagogue' verb
(*sunago*) when he writes to the church in Corinth:
'When you are *assembled* [synagogued, gathered
together] in the name of the Lord Jesus . . .' (1 Cor. 5:4).
The Christian church is an assembly in the name of the
Lord Jesus. The local church is the concrete expression
in this age of the gathering by God of his people. It is
the Temple of the Holy Spirit, the place on earth where
God lives, the community of Jesus to which the
Tabernacle in the desert and the Temple in Jerusalem
pointed (1 Cor. 3:9,16; 1 Pet. 2:5).

The Local Church: Genetic Blueprint of a Remade World

We shall now explore seven elements of the genetic blueprint of a reassembled world, each of which is to be
found in the authentic local church.

A. *Gathered by grace*

The local church is an assembly for access to God by the
death of Jesus. We have seen repeatedly (and especially
in Chapters 1 and 2) the fundamental reason why human
relationships are so fragile and broken is our fellowship
with God has been broken by sin: that we are, in the language of Genesis 3, excluded from the garden of Eden.
Access to God is therefore the precondition for the
re-establishment of stable human harmony.

The Assembly of Israel at Sinai was an ambiguous
anticipation of this access. Although the LORD 'came
down' and was present amongst his people, they were
absolutely forbidden to draw near to him. It was an
assembly at a distance. So let us go back to the passage
in Hebrews 12 where the writer says Christian assemblies are coming to the heavenly Jerusalem rather than
coming to Sinai (vv. 18–29). The writer of this letter is
very keen to encourage his readers to keep on meeting.
'Let us not give up meeting together, as some are in the
habit of doing, but let us encourage one another – and all
the more as you see the Day approaching' (10:25).

One of the ways he encourages them near the end of
his letter is to lift their eyes to understand what they are
doing when they meet with their brothers and sisters. In
this magnificent passage he contrasts the assembly at
Sinai with the New Covenant assembly at 'the heavenly
Jerusalem'. 'You have not come to' Sinai, he says, with a

vivid description of the sheer terror of that assembly (vv. 18–21). I take it that when the writer says, 'You have not come . . . You have come . . .' (vv. 18,22), he speaks of the heavenly assembly as it is expressed tangibly in our local church assemblies. He is not speaking just of individual Christians coming in some mystical way to the heavenly Jerusalem, but very concretely of their local church meetings. So, if a local church meeting is not terrifying like Sinai, what is it?

> But you have come to Mount Zion, to the heavenly Jerusalem, the city of the living God. You have come to thousands upon thousands of angels in joyful assembly, to the church of the firstborn, whose names are written in heaven. You have come to God, the judge of all men, to the spirits of righteous men made perfect, to Jesus the mediator of a new covenant, and to the sprinkled blood that speaks a better word than the blood of Abel. (12:22–24)

He is filled with joyful adoration because we have *not* come to Sinai. Thank God, he says, we have not come to that place of terror, distance and forbidden access.

However, in at least four ways the local church assembly *is* like Sinai, and we ought to note these before we look at the differences. First, it is still an assembly! Second, it is still an assembly in the presence of God (we come 'to God, the judge of all men', v. 23). Third, the God in whose presence we assemble is still 'a consuming fire' (v. 29), just as he always was and always will be. Fourth, we still assemble to hear and heed his word ('See to it that you do not refuse him who speaks' v. 25).

But the place has moved (in Bible imagery) from Sinai to Zion, to the place where the blood of the Covenant has been shed, to the place where the mediator of a better Covenant welcomes us, takes us by the hand and brings us to God (1 Pet. 3:18). This is now the place where we draw near with confidence. It is no longer a gathering for distance, but an assembly for access.

The key to the access available in this assembly is the contrast in verse 24 between 'the blood of Abel' and 'the sprinkled blood that speaks a better word than the blood of Abel'. The blood of Abel 'cries out' from the ground for God to act in judgment upon Cain; it 'speaks' by crying out for just judgment upon Cain and upon all sinners (Gen. 4:10). If the only 'sound' God hears is the blood of Abel, then all of us are doomed to destruction. We cannot access a holy God without being burned alive by the consuming fire of his justice.

By contrast with this, 'the sprinkled blood' reminds us of the blood of the covenant sacrifice sprinkled by Moses on the people (Exod. 24:6–8). It also reminds us of the blood of the Passover Lamb saving the firstborn from death: so 'the church of the firstborn' (v. 23) seems to refer back to the Passover. The Passover was also in the writer's mind in 11:28: 'By faith [Moses] kept the Passover and the sprinkling of the blood, so that the destroyer of the firstborn would not touch the firstborn of Israel'.

The 'blood' of the Passover and the Covenant foreshadowed the death of a sacrifice in our place, and the 'sprinkled blood' speaks of the benefits of that death being applied to us. The wonderful thing about the local church assembly is that it is the one 'place' on earth where men and women can now have access to God as they gather in the name of Jesus and trust in his death for them. Now at last the cherubim can be 'stood down' from their vital job as the 'bouncers' on the door of the Garden of Eden; now a violent thief can be promised that on the day of his execution he will be with Jesus in the garden; now men and women can be reconciled to God and stand in the grace won for them by the Cross (Luke 23:43; Rom. 5:1–11).

B. Humbled under grace

Our self-perception as Christians deeply affects whether or not Christ builds an authentic church through us. Who I am determines the friends I make. That's a simple principle every teacher sees at work in the school playground: you see a teenager unsure of her identity, wandering unstably from group to group. Will she be a conformist or a rebel, with the trendy or the plain, the steady or the wild, the goths or the geeks? Then she makes her decision, and you know the decision she has taken because of the group to which she now belongs, where she hangs out. Who I am determines where I belong. Identity shapes community, self-perception forms fellowship. In order to be accepted by a social group I must line up my self and my identity with their character.

This simple principle holds not only in the playground, but with every human community, and it holds in the local church. The character of the local church is moulded by the self-perception of its members. Who we think we are individually will shape the fellowship we form and the people who join us.

East of Eden perhaps the most obvious cause of separation and scattering is pride. This is why when Jesus builds his church he must first destroy pride. Pride was the mindset of the builders of the Tower of Babel. The first thing that the gospel of the cross does is to humble us deeply under grace. In a crucial passage in the letter to the Romans, Paul teaches them what Jesus did on the cross and how this makes it possible for guilty men and women to be in right relationship with God (Rom.

3:21–26). Immediately after this, he tells them the 'so what?' of this truth: 'Where, then, is boasting? It is excluded' (v. 27). In the context of Romans, the boasting in Paul's mind is probably the boasting of the religious person who thinks he or she is on a higher level than others in the church. But the point is simple: if the only way I can be reconciled to God is for Jesus to die for me, and if I am not able to make any contribution at all to my justification, it follows I had no cause of boasting, have no reason to boast, and can never ever have even the slightest reason to feel pleased with myself and superior to others. The pride of Babel is utterly undermined by the gospel of the cross. There are no tower-builders in Eden.

Any gathering based upon anything we have done, any of our achievements, any of our privileges or any tribal markers of belonging is doomed to scattering, because it is rooted in human pride. Those who belong to such a gathering do so because of some merit or privilege in them. It will therefore inevitably degenerate into what someone has called a 'prig sty', a place for stuck-up prigs who are proud to belong. Such a community will always be riven with splits as one group and another, or one individual or another, make bids for supremacy and priority.

Another way of saying we are humbled under grace is to say we are to be 'like children'. In Matthew 16 Jesus says he is going to build his church, that is, to gather together his assembly (v. 18). In Matthew 18 he speaks to his disciples about what kind of gathering they will be. Matthew 18 begins with a question about status: 'Who is the greatest in the kingdom of heaven?' (v. 1). This is not a question that has gone away in the history of the church: how can I use the church to gain status?

Before Jesus states anything, he calls for his visual aid, a child. He stands him in the middle of the disciples, pauses, and says, 'I want you to grasp, because this is important, that unless you turn your attitudes 180 degrees around and become like children, you won't enter the kingdom. Never mind having status, you won't even get past the front door. But if you become like a kid then you will have real substantial status in the kingdom' (vv. 3,4).

What does Jesus mean by saying his followers must become 'like little children'? He does not mean children are innocent. Some years ago I read a newspaper report in which police called at a house to arrest a teenager suspected of shoplifting. His mother and teenage sister said he wasn't at home. But his toddler brother blurted out, 'Oh, yes, he is. He's hiding in the wardrobe!' The policeman commented later to the press that this showed 'children that age can only tell the truth; and that is nice.' Well, it would be nice, if it were true. But I can only conclude that that policeman was neither a father nor an uncle nor a teacher, nor had ever had anything to do with real children. Children are not innocent. Nor does Jesus mean that children are trusting. They may be; they may not. Kids can be deeply and healthily suspicious, especially of strangers. Nor does Jesus mean that, as one commentary claims, children are, 'untempted to self-advancement'. This is a strange idea and reminds me of the man who wrote in his autobiography, apparently unaware of the irony: 'I have never lost the childlike humility which characterizes all truly great men.'

No, the point about a child is not some supposed subjective virtue. It is the child is objectively, in terms of status and the perception of society, a nobody. The question Jesus was asked was about status; the answer he gives is about status. The child is to be looked after, not looked up to. The child is weak, yes, vulnerable, yes, and – in first century Jewish society, pretty much despised.

Attitudes in Jesus' day would be more like that of Kingsley Amis, who said, 'It was no wonder that people were so horrible, when they started life as children', or Nancy Mitford, who said, 'I love children – especially when they cry, for then someone takes them away.' You did not hold on to childhood in Jesus' culture, like Peter Pan: you longed to grow up, to become a full voting member of society, to be treated with respect, and so on.

So to turn and humble yourself like a child is not to take on the supposed sweet innocent self-effacing humble mindset of the child: that is an imagined construction of the romantic mind. No, it is to accept the status of the child, to grasp and accept I have no status. I am a nobody. I bring nothing with me into the kingdom. I must expect the world to look down on me, much as I would prefer them to look up.

This is what Jesus did. When Jesus humbled himself, he did not become innocent having previously been guilty; nor did he stop seeking advancement when he previously had; nor become trusting when he had formerly been suspicious (Phil. 2:8). Instead, he took the status of a despised human being, when he had previously lived in glory. He was born to an unmarried mother, hunted by Herod in infancy, lived in despised Nazareth (John 1:46; 7:42), baptized with sinners, followed by fishermen, with nowhere to lay his head, misunderstood and rejected by his own family, and finally hounded to a shameful and undeserved death.

Only the message of grace can so humble you and me that we cease to be driven by the divisive desire for status in the church. The desire for status divides and scatters. Only grace unites.

The story is told in the 1820s in England of a Holy Communion service in a village church, at which the Duke of Wellington was present. In those years after the battle of Waterloo, the duke was the greatest citizen in the country, under the king, sometime prime minister and a man of very great status. The expectation was the duke would take communion on his own first, and only then would the bread and wine be given to the rest of the congregation. But by some misunderstanding, a common farm worker found himself alongside the duke waiting for the bread and wine. The poor man was very embarrassed and made as if to return to his seat, when the duke motioned him to stay, and said, 'We are all equal here.' I don't know if the duke really said that, but if he did, he was absolutely right! The church of Jesus Christ ought to be a place where all desire for status and all arrogant scrambling for it, is eliminated by the gospel of the cross. By this humbling a broken world will be remade.

C. Inclusive by grace

A consequence of this humbling is the authentic local church will welcome anyone, no matter what their race, education, culture or status in the eyes of the world. The logic is we come into the kingdom as nobodies, and because we all know that we have no status we ourselves will willingly welcome other nobodies to join us. Or, to be precise, we will recognize Jesus has already welcomed other nobodies to join us, and we will reflect his welcome in the welcome we too extend to them.

This logic is evident in the same passage in Matthew 18. Immediately after saying his disciples must 'change and become like little children', Jesus says, 'whoever welcomes a little child like this in my name welcomes me. But if anyone causes one of these little ones who believe in me to sin, it would be better for him to have a large millstone hung around his neck and be drowned in the depths of the sea' (vv. 4–6). The 'little one' is the same as the 'child', a metaphor for the Christian of any age (hence the explanation 'who believe in me'). If we have not turned and become like children, accepting zero status, then we will treat applicants for membership in the way any human club treats applicants: we will ask if they can step up and meet the entrance requirements, if they qualify to belong. We will cause them to stumble at the church door, turning them away in our pride unless they are people like us.

But with Jesus it was so different: because Jesus had no status, he attracted to himself men and women who had no status. His group was defined by the negation of human status: therefore the least, the lost and the last were drawn to him like parched men to water.

When I walk in Jesus' footsteps and become 'like a child' I will willingly receive 'a child' into my group. Only when my self-perception is that I am a despised nobody will I welcome other despised nobodies into my fellowship. Only when I myself am deeply humbled will my door be open to the lost, the struggling and the desperate.

If we do not receive nobodies, we do not receive Jesus Christ. That is why putting up barriers of pride is so serious. That is why it would be better to have a quick and early death by drowning than to do something like that. That is why it is so desperately important a church be a church of 'children', a church in which status is zero and agreed to be zero and proclaimed to be zero.

This is so different to the religion of the Pharisees. In Matthew 23 Jesus condemns them for laying heavy burdens on the people. They get their praise from one another, the religious people. They get their status from their praying or their generous giving or their fasting, their zeal and public piety (as in Matt. 6). In particular,

Jesus says to them they shut the kingdom of heaven in people's faces (v. 13), because (a) they themselves do not enter (they don't become like children), and therefore (b) they do not allow those who would enter to go in. That is to say, they won't become like children and therefore they won't receive 'children'. They put a stumbling block in the way. And so Jesus says the tax collectors and prostitutes go in to the kingdom before them (Matt. 21:31), because these no-hopers grasp that they are nobodies and therefore exactly the people Jesus wants to gather.

The church of Jesus Christ is inclusive by grace. This is a hard thing to be, because it is so against the values of the world, and the world will despise us for it. By nature every human community is like an economic trade area that places a tariff barrier around it. You may join us, but only if you pay, only if you can manage the tariff. By nature every church is like this. We'd love you to join our club, but only if you become like us. But Jesus proclaims a community that undermines all tariff barriers. It is a community, a fellowship, with no moral tariff barrier to entry, a society with open doors to receive anyone who will turn and abandon self-righteousness, or pride in status, and come empty-handed to the foot of the Cross of Christ, and then be changed by grace.

The only person who will be excluded from the church is the one who thinks he or she has no need of grace. Only pride, or proud impenitence, can keep someone outside. The assembly of Jesus Christ has no step that someone has to step up to get in: but it has a very low gate, so that only those who abandon self-righteousness and status will bow low enough to come in. People are excluded not by being too low, but by thinking themselves too high. This welcoming inclusiveness of grace is the seed of a remade world.

Another place where this barrier-breaking dynamic of the local church is seen is Paul's letter to the Ephesians. The message of grace proclaims we can contribute nothing at all to being rescued: it follows that anyone anywhere in the world can be rescued, and will be rescued only through the kindness of God in Jesus at the cross. This message is not tied to one particular ethnic group, one language group, one social class or one culture.

> 'For he himself [Jesus] is our peace, who has made the two one and has destroyed the barrier, the dividing wall of hostility, by abolishing in his flesh the law with its commandments and regulations. His purpose was to create in himself one new man out of the two, thus making peace, and in this one body to reconcile both of them to God through the cross, by which he put to death their hostility. He came and preached peace to you who were far away and peace to those who were near. For through him we both have access to the Father by one Spirit. (Eph. 2:14–18)

It matters deeply that the local assembly of a Christian church does not exclude anyone on grounds of race, culture or class. To do so is a denial of the gospel of grace. There was a dramatic showdown over this issue very early in the life of the young Christian churches, in Antioch, the first city where the gospel was shared with Gentiles (Acts 11:20). Jews and Gentiles were, amazingly, eating together as a sign they had been brought together in Jesus by the cross. But then a group of conservative Jews from Jerusalem arrived and started eating separately. Even the apostle Peter succumbed to pressure to eat separately, and Paul courageously challenged him, realizing that the gospel itself was at stake.

When Peter came to Antioch, I opposed him to his face, because he was clearly in the wrong. Before certain men came from James, he used to eat with the Gentiles. But when they arrived, he began to draw back and separate himself from the Gentiles because he was afraid of those who belonged to the circumcision group. The other Jews joined him in his hypocrisy, so that by their hypocrisy even Barnabas was led astray.

When I saw that they were not acting in line with the truth of the gospel, I said to Peter in front of them all, "You are a Jew, yet you live like a Gentile and not like a Jew. How is it, then, that you force Gentiles to follow Jewish customs? We who are Jews by birth and not 'Gentile sinners' know that a man is not justified by observing the law, but by faith in Jesus Christ. So we, too, have put our faith in Christ Jesus that we may be justified by faith in Christ and not by observing the law, because by observing the law no one will be justified." (Gal. 2:11–16)

To impose any kind of cultural bar to fellowship is 'not acting in line with the truth of the gospel' (v. 14) and must be stopped. The local church ought to be the one place in a society where the deepest divides begin to be bridged. But this cannot be achieved by social engineering, or by exhortation from church leaders: it happens only as the grace of God in Jesus is preached repeatedly and applied practically in every area of church life.

It is worth saying that we cannot make any of our churches perfectly multicultural. There are all sorts of reasons why our local churches will often tend to be dominated by one particular culture, not least because they are local and reflect the culture(s) of the localities in which they are placed (and, of course, they have to choose which language to conduct their meetings in). We must not beat ourselves because our churches are not perfectly mixed. When Jesus builds his church he starts with very broken materials. The key is we are consciously and deliberately seeking to see the message of grace break down barriers. It is not so much where our churches have got to that matters, but what direction they are moving in.

D. Connected by grace

I have spoken of the 'local church'. Some will wonder where a denomination fits in to the picture, such as the Church of England, the Baptist Union, or the Presbyterian Church of America, or an Association, Connection or Fellowship of churches, such as the Fellowship of Independent Evangelical Churches. It is important to be clear that when the New Testament writers address 'the church' in a particular place, they write to what we would call a local church (or possibly a small group of churches in the same locality). The word 'church' in the New Testament usually means either a local church or the universal church (all people who belong to Christ, from every age and every place).

The local church recognizes it is one of a large number of worldwide scattered gatherings. This means a strong awareness that no one local church stands alone. We are part of a global movement of God which is not aimed at just producing separate local gatherings, but will in the end lead to one worldwide people. Paul starts 1 Corinthians by writing, 'To the church of God in Corinth', that is, he writes to one local gathering. But he goes on to describe them as 'sanctified in Christ Jesus and called to be holy' (that is, set apart to belong to Christ and called to behave in a 'set apart' way) *'together with all those everywhere who call on the name of our Lord Jesus Christ – their Lord and ours'*

(1:2). Wherever we gather, we are to remember our spiritual identity is shared with all those everywhere who call on the name of Jesus. Our experience will be different in detail, but similar in essentials to that of all Christians everywhere (see, e.g., 1 Thess. 2:14; 1 Pet. 5:9).

We ought not to be dogmatic about exactly how this awareness of worldwide fellowship will manifest itself in a local church. There are all sorts of ways, both formal and informal, in which this interlinked fellowship is expressed. But the important thing is an individual local church remembers that we are part of a much bigger movement of God, by which he will gather in men and women from all over the world into one flock under one Shepherd (John 10:16).

E. Secure in grace

The local church is a people who are secure and satisfied in the God of grace. Like the Jerusalem of Old Testament promise, the church is the place of security in a broken-world. James the brother of Jesus addresses the problem of quarrelling in a surprising way:

> What causes fights and quarrels among you? Don't they come from your desires that battle within you? You want something but don't get it. You kill and covet, but you cannot have what you want. You quarrel and fight.

Why do they quarrel? Because they covet and cannot get what they want. So what is the remedy for covetousness?

> You do not have, because you do not ask God. When you ask, you do not receive, because you ask with wrong motives, that you may spend what you get on your pleasures. (Jas 4:1–3)

They quarrel because they covet and cannot have what they want: they do not have because they do not ask God, and even when they do ask God, they ask just so they can enjoy their selfish pleasures. That is, they want to use God like a magic wand to help them get what they want. James goes on to say they need to repent and humble themselves before God (4:4–10). Only when they learn to find their satisfaction in the grace God loves to pour out (v. 6) will they learn contentment.

In the same way, the writer to the Hebrews answers the love of money with the promise and sufficiency of God.

> Keep your lives free from the love of money and be content with what you have, because God has said,
> "Never will I leave you;
> never will I forsake you." (Heb. 13:5)

The authentic local church is a place where men and women are beginning to learn to find their identity and security in the God of promise and grace. This safe grace is the root answer to human desires that lead to quarrelling, discontent and division. In this way too the local church contains within itself the seeds of a remade world.

F. Forgiving through grace

The local church is an assembly able to stay together in harmony because they forgive as the Lord forgave them. Forgiveness is a vital element in the cure for scattering. The only safe dynamic that can unlock unlimited forgiveness is the gospel of the cross. Paul writes to the Colossians,

Therefore, as God's chosen people, holy and dearly loved, clothe yourselves with compassion, kindness, humility, gentleness and patience. Bear with each other and forgive whatever grievances you may have against one another. *Forgive as the Lord forgave you.* (3:12,13)

We can only forgive freely when we know deeply we have been forgiven freely. Few things divide and scatter human beings as deeply as unforgiveness. Many marriages end up being broken not by the bad behaviour of one party but by the refusal of the other to forgive. Only the gospel of free scandalous forgiveness can set us free to offer free scandalous forgiveness to others, and therefore to continue to live in fellowship with them in spite of their, and our, sinfulness.

Let us return to Matthew 18 and see how Jesus unlocks this dynamic in the parable of the unforgiving servant (vv. 21–35). It is a shocking passage, for at the end of it the person tortured for eternity is not an offender but a victim. A man who is wronged at the start (by an unpaid debt) ends up tortured at the end. This is such a horrifying scenario we had better look carefully at what is going on, because the Lord Jesus Christ teaches us this is how things will actually be. The context of the parable is a block of teaching to the disciples (all of Matt. 18) in which Jesus teaches how he will build his church. We have seen he first demolishes pride by teaching we must become 'like little children'. We must be nobodies, and welcome nobodies. Verses 15 to 20 address the problem when a believer sins and persistently will not repent. Now Jesus comes to the – in some ways harder – question of what to do if they sin and do repent, again and again! Each time they cause pain within the fellowship they repent, but they go on doing it.

That is Peter's question in verse 21. It is so typical of Peter to ask the question that needs to be asked. 'Lord, how many times shall I forgive my brother when he sins against me?' The implication is the Christian brother or sister does repent, because if they won't repent, then verses 15 to 17 tell us what to do. And in the closely parallel passage in Luke 17:3,4 Jesus says, 'If your brother sins, rebuke him, and if he repents, forgive him, and if he sins against you seven times in a day and seven times comes back to you and says, "I repent," forgive him.' So the implication here is forgiveness can only effectively be offered and received by one who repents. But what are the limits of offered forgiveness? What if he does repent?

In some ways this is even harder than if he doesn't. For our hearts are such it is somehow gratifying to press on with the process of verses 15 to 17. When the door is finally shut on this impenitent offender and he is locked out of the fellowship, we feel he had it coming to him, he got his just deserts, and it served him right. There is something satisfying about that! Everyone can see I was the victim, and he was the offender, and now he is punished, as offenders should be.

But what if he repents? Well, of course I must forgive him the first time, and the second, and I guess, to stretch a point, the third. There was a tradition in the rabbis that three times was about right. But after that I must conclude that his repentance is not genuine, whatever he says, mustn't I? I can't go on forgiving. Peter is generous. How about 'seven times' he suggests? That's a lot (and a biblical symbolic number of completeness), and it echoes Luke 17:4.

Jesus says, 'Peter, I don't think you've understood the meaning of "seven".' When I say that if he sins and repents seven times you must forgive him, I didn't mean 'seven' as a mathematical number, but as a number that means 'on and on and on'. We would say infinity. No, I do not say to you seven times, but seventy times seven – or it may be seventy-seven, but the meaning is the same, on and on and on without limit.

Seventy-seven is precisely how revenge works. In Chapter 1 we met Lamech with his boast of revenge: 'If Cain's revenge is sevenfold, then Lamech's is seventy-sevenfold' (Gen. 4:24). The word for 'seventy-seven' in the Greek translation of the Old Testament is the same as the word Jesus uses here in Matthew 18:22. Jesus says he wants his church to be the place where the world's disproportionate retaliation is turned upside down and becomes outrageously disproportionate forgiveness. At the end of the parable (v. 35) he says this is not an optional extra: unless this limitless heartfelt forgiveness is forthcoming, the heavenly Father won't forgive us. James says the same: 'judgment without mercy will be shown to anyone who has not been merciful' (2:13).

However, the important point for the church is to grasp the logic of the extraordinary parable in verses 23 to 35. A servant owes his king 'ten thousand talents'. A few years before Jesus told this story, the total annual revenue of Galilee, Perea, Judea, Samaria and Idumaea, was about 800 talents. The amount he owes the king exceeds the total money in circulation in the whole country at the time. 'Ten thousand' was the biggest number in the Greek language; and the talent was the biggest unit of currency. So we might say, he owed the king trillions of pounds, dollars or euros. It is an astronomical debt. Astonishingly, the king releases him from this debt. The servant then meets a fellow servant who owes him 'a hundred denarii'. A denarius was about a day's wage for a labourer so this was not a trivial debt: it was more than three months' wages.[58] He will not forgive. We know the rest of the story.

The logic of the story is this: the only dynamic that will unlock forgiveness in human community is a deep understanding of the astronomical debt which God has forgiven us in Christ. It would be quite unreasonable to expect the servant to release his fellow-servant from a debt of three months' wages, *except that we know* that he himself had first been released from a debt of several hundred thousand years' worth of wages. Only the gospel of the cross will bring this understanding deeply into our hearts: and therefore only the gospel of the cross can unlock really costly and supernatural forgiveness of a kind able to really remake a broken world.

G. Suffering through grace

The final mark by which the local church has the seeds of remaking a broken world I want to note is a surprising one: we exist and function in weakness rather than power. We are a society who follow a Master who suffered in weakness and refused to use power to defend himself, because the source of his kingly power was not worldly force. He said to Pontius Pilate, 'My kingdom is not of this world', which means that the source of his authority was not from this world. '*If it were, my servants would fight* to prevent my arrest by the Jews' (John 18:36). Fighting, the exercise of all the power and force we can muster, is the way the world acts. But Jesus overcame evil with good and calls his followers to do the same (Rom. 12:21). The local church is therefore to be a body of men and women who live in the world in weakness, who expect to be wronged and ill-treated, and who are learning not to hit back because they follow the one who, when he was insulted, did not retaliate, and when he suffered, made no threats (1 Pet. 2:23).

This is an extraordinary way to behave, but it is the only way that can remake a broken world. This is quite different from the ways of Babylon: and yet the only force that can overcome Babylon is the force of weakness, the power of the cross. Babylon has no answer to this. So often in human revolutions an injustice is overcome by the greater power of what turns into a greater injustice. When this happens, all that happens is that one evil is replaced by another evil. Evil can only be overcome by good. Only a people confident of the grace of God can entrust themselves, as Jesus did, to the God who judges justly (1 Pet. 2:23).

The Local Church is a Mixture of Jerusalem and Babylon

These seven marks of the authentic local church are indeed the genetic blueprint for reassembling a fractured world. A society which is gathered by grace, humbled under grace, inclusive under grace, secure in grace, connected world-wide by grace, forgiving by grace and willing to suffer in grace will be a powerful force for harmony. They would be Jerusalem on earth in all her beauty.

Sadly, however, we have to recognize every actual local church on earth is a mixture of Jerusalem and Babylon. If a church is defined and driven by the word of God preached in the power of the Spirit, then we may expect all these seven wonderful marks to be evident. But they will be evident in the midst of all the contradictory markers of Babylon. Humility will be mixed with pride, harmony spoiled by division, security undermined by people trying to prove themselves, connectedness undone by a parochial defensiveness, forgiveness neutered by resentments, and weakness replaced by worldly power-plays.

Real Christianity can become debased and become
nothing better than any human religion. The history of
Christian denominations seeking institutional unity
epitomizes this problem. An article describing a pro-
posed reunification of two branches of the Russian
Orthodox church commented the disputes that lay
behind the split they were seeking to heal were, 'only
one example of a paradox in the recent history of
[Christianity]. Almost every time two Christian communities – split by politics, race, culture or doctrine –
decide to reunite, a new division is created by those who
cannot accept the merger.'[59] Real Christian churches are
not Jerusalem here on earth!

So we need to consider the kinds of ways in which the
authentic grace-shaped gathering of the local church can
be replaced by some kind of pseudo-church, that calls
itself church but is actually not the genuine article. There
are plenty of gatherings both in the Bible and in human
history that are counterfeit imitations of the spiritual
gathering of the people of God. In their different ways
they all take us back to Babel. Let us consider some of
them.

A. Counterfeit church: the idolatrous assembly

Even while the people of Israel were assembled by God
at Sinai, they managed to transform their assembly from
one of true worship into one of idolatry.

> When the people saw that Moses was so long in coming
> down from the mountain, they gathered round Aaron and
> said, "Come, make us gods . . ." (Exod. 32:1)

This was a kind of assembly (they 'gathered round
Aaron'). But it was not an assembly gathered by and

under the word of God. On the contrary, it was an assembly of human initiative called in order to produce some gods shaped by human imagination. Any religious gathering not shaped week by week by the preaching of the word of God will revert to becoming an idolatrous assembly, in which human tradition or imagination will begin to shape gods made in our image. One of the tests of authentic gospel assembly is the questions they ask when they want to call or appoint a new pastor or leader. Do they ask, 'Preach to us the word God has spoken'? Or is their agenda actually that he will work with them to produce a god shaped the way they would like god to be, perhaps the therapeutic god whose mission is to meet my needs and make me feel better?

Any 'church' that in practice worships a god shaped by human desires will be a divisive rather than a uniting force in society, for it will inevitably be shaped by its own longings in a way that will bring it into conflict with other societies or communities, shaped in turn by their own prejudices, interests or desires.

B. Counterfeit church: the self-righteous assembly

The prophets in the Old Testament sometimes looked at the gatherings of Israel and observed they did nothing to change people's lives. These people met together in the name of God (we would call them a 'church'), but there was no inner life-changing reality to correspond to what they said. They had 'the form of godliness' but denied 'its power' (2 Tim. 3:5). Of this kind of empty gathering, that just makes religious people feel better about themselves, God says,

> 'I cannot bear your evil assemblies.' (Isa. 1:13)
> 'I cannot stand your assemblies.' (Amos 5:21)

This kind of 'church' always metamorphoses into a church of Pharisees. If my life is not being changed by the word of God in daily repentance and fresh faith, the alternative is I will be affirmed in my sinfulness and just end up feeling better and better about myself. This will always make me look down on others, and make the 'church' a divisive force in society. Only when the church consists of men and women being humbled and changed by grace will it be the kind of society that welcomes other needy people in.

C. Counterfeit church: the homogeneous assembly

The third kind of gathering that may look like a Christian church but is not, is an assembly that defines itself by some homogeneous cultural boundaries. It is clear, for example, from Galatians or Ephesians, Paul would not have recognized as a church any assembly that defined itself as either Jewish or Gentile and did not allow the other category of person to belong, and indeed welcome them. What happens then is a church metamorphoses into a club.

In some circumstances there is nothing wrong with a club. A sports club will welcome into membership those who play that sport, for example. In some way a club is defined by human talents (e.g. sport), human achievement (e.g. the wealth to pay the subscription) or human culture (e.g. a club for expatriates from one country in another). But a church is not a club. A church by definition welcomes any man or woman who will accept the free grace of God. A church must welcome a penitent murderer, a repentant member of a despised race or nation and a dropout and morally messed-up person who comes to his senses in the far country and returns to the Father God (Luke 15:11–24).

D. Counterfeit church: the hostile assembly

Finally, the Bible observes a consistent pattern that one of the few things that will unite men and women without God is having God as their common enemy! In Numbers 16 Korah and his followers 'banded [assembled] together' not because they were gathered by God but precisely 'against the LORD' (Num. 16:11). Psalm 2 pictures a great international alliance against God and his anointed Christ:

> The kings of the earth take their stand
> and the rulers gather together
> against the LORD
> and against his Anointed One [Messiah, Christ]. (v. 2)

The anti-God archetypal alliance of Psalm 2 is fulfilled in the united hostility against Jesus. Immediately after quoting this psalm the disciples go on to say:

> Indeed Herod and Pontius Pilate met together with the Gentiles and the people of Israel in this city to conspire against your holy servant Jesus, whom you anointed [i.e. the Messiah of Psalm 2:2][60]

In New Testament times King Herod wasn't generally friends with anyone, and yet paradoxically he found himself ganging up both with the Pharisees and later with Pontius Pilate against Jesus:

> Then the Pharisees went out and began to plot with the Herodians how they might kill Jesus. (Mark 3:6; and see also Mark 12:13 for the same surprising alliance)

> That day [when Jesus was on trial] Herod and Pilate became friends—before this they had been enemies. (Luke 23:12)

The same Psalm 2 anti-Christ alliance is precisely what the disciples face under persecution in Acts 4:

> The next day the rulers, elders and teachers of the law met in Jerusalem. Annas the high priest was there, and so were Caiaphas, John, Alexander and the other men of the high priest's family. (vv. 5–6)

Right through the story of Acts, the most bitter hostility to the gospel of grace comes from religious people, whether they be jealous Jews in the synagogues who feared the loss of religious power and influence or pagan idolaters.[61]

Conclusion: Persevere with the Mixed Experience of the Local Church

One of the paradoxes of contemporary culture is two apparently contradictory things are often said about religion. On the one hand, it is frequently said all religions are essentially the same. I am told somewhere near Chicago there is a Bahai temple in which there is a central altar, from which nine aisles radiate like the spokes of a wheel from the hub. At the end of each aisle there is a little archway and each archway is dedicated to a different religious leader, each representing one of the world's religions. It doesn't matter which archway you enter through, basically you are doing the same thing and going to the same place.

And yet people also say religion is a very divisive influence in the world. But here's a puzzle: if religions are basically the same, how come they are so divisive? Or, to put it the other way, if they are so divisive, how come they haven't recognized they are all the same? The answer is at a deep level they are all the same: but their sameness is 'Tower of Babel' sameness rather than gospel sameness! Of course, there are enormous differences between the world's religions: for example, Buddhists do not really believe in god at all, whereas Hindus believe in many gods and goddesses. But beneath these differences they all affirm human initiative in religion and therefore puff up human pride. They are not rescue religions, religions of pure grace. At the centre of that Bahai temple there ought not to be an altar (symbolizing access to God), but a boxing ring, since all that happens when human religions collide is strife. Only the gospel of pure grace can humble human beings and gather them together in love.

The assembly of the local church can so easily degenerate into being just a manifestation of another human religion yet carrying the 'Christian' label. When a church degenerates like this it will usually show elements of some or all of these counterfeit assemblies. We must be realistic about this. And yet in the midst of all this disappointment, we must not lose sight of the wonderful fact that where the gospel of grace is preached, the seven marks of a community that will rebuild a broken world will also be found.

If therefore we can join, belong and serve in such a fellowship, we will do well to do so. We will find ourselves to be a part of God's supernatural international plan to rebuild a broken world. The precise ways in which we serve as a part of this plan will vary enormously. For most Christians it will be a case of just belonging and serving wholeheartedly in a local church shaped by the word of God. Some will be sent out as missionaries in other cultures, or indeed in their own culture (perhaps as teachers in schools where they can reach others for Christ), and the constraints of their missionary work will limit their immediate involvement in a local church: but always they will have their eyes on the aim of seeing local churches built, men and women not just made into individualistic disciples but integrated into local church life as soon as possible. For a few, service of the local church may mean involvement in some para-church movement such as Christian Unions in schools or universities: but again, those of us who do this will always make sure that our para-church involvement really is serving the local church rather than seeking to upstage or replace it – for it is the local church, these wonderful scattered gatherings, which God is using to rebuild a broken world. In our final chapter we lift our sights to see where the local church is heading.

Questions for Discussion

1. In this chapter, how do we see God use the terrible scattering of persecution to bring about gathering of peoples from all over the world?
2. What seven elements did we note of the genetic blueprint of a reassembled world?
3. How can we make sure we are churches humbled under grace, and avoid worldly hierarchies and seeking after status? How do concerns about status creep into church life?
4. In particular, how can we honour the role of church leaders without giving them worldly status?
5. Review the section 'Inclusive by grace'. What should be the criterion used to decide whether or not someone is welcomed into a church fellowship? What other criteria do we mistakenly use?
6. What are the differences (in terms of human relationships) between a church splitting because of

disagreements and a church sending out missionaries or a church-planting team? How do these differences show the difference between scattering as a sign of God's judgment and the creation of new 'scattered gatherings'?

7. How can our churches build a sense of being part of a worldwide movement of God to remake a broken world?

8. How can we model a joyful contentment in God in the midst of an insecure world?

9. Think carefully to see if there are any people whom you need to forgive and have not forgiven, even though they have repented. Take to heart what Jesus teaches about how much God has forgiven you, and offer them forgiveness.

10. How do worldly attitudes towards wielding influence in society creep into Christian circles? How can we make sure we overcome evil only with good, and use the power of weakness rather than worldly strength?

11. Review the four types of counterfeit assembly we noted in this chapter. What warning signs might there be that a church is becoming one of these? How can we guard against this happening?

Section D

The New Creation:
Gathering Consummated

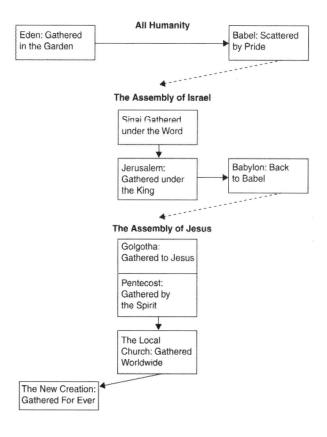

9

The New Creation: Gathered Forever

God's Master Plan

Near the start of his letter to the Ephesians, the Apostle Paul tells us something of great importance and wonder. He introduces it with a sustained build up: 'And he [God] made known to us [the apostles] the mystery of his will' – that is, what he wanted and had decided to do, which had been hidden in Old Testament types and shadows, but has now been revealed – 'according to his good pleasure' – this is what is really close to his heart – 'to be put into effect when the times will have reached their fulfilment . . .' It is quite a build up! So what is this decision and plan of God, known in shadowy form in the Old Testament, revealed clearly to the apostles and for us in the New Testament, waiting to be finalized at the end of time? It is 'to bring all things in heaven and on earth together under one head, even Christ' (Eph. 1:9,10). What God has decided to do, longs to do, and will most certainly do at the end of time, is to gather together a broken world and rebuild it under one leader, the Lord Jesus Christ. This finally will be the keeping of the promise to Abraham that through his descendant he would rule the world and inherit the earth. This is the fulfilment of all those prophecies, such as Ezekiel 34 to 37, that God would put one shepherd, his servant David, over one united flock (see pp. 123–127). This at last will be the gathering to end all scatterings; and it will be cosmic in its scope.

Some while ago my family gave me a wonderful spherical jigsaw for my birthday. It was made of 500 rigid plastic curved pieces, and it made the globe of the world, painted with seas and countries, mountains, trade routes, longitude and latitude lines, and so on. We started with the pieces strewn over the floor, broken and scattered. My daughter and daughter-in-law helped me put it together: the feeling of satisfaction when we slipped the North Pole into place at the end was terrific: we had remade a broken globe! It had been scattered, and we had gathered it. I guess that feeling of delight is just a very pale echo of the glorious delight God will have on that day when he finally brings all things in heaven and on earth together under Jesus Christ. That is our subject in this final chapter.

The Bible in three acts

We saw at the start the Bible story can be told in three acts. Act I (Gen. 1 and 2) is the original created harmony of heaven and earth, one coherent creation, where the will of God is done equally on earth and in heaven and there is no divide or curtain between the two. Act II (most of the rest of the Bible story) recounts the separation of earth from heaven and the consequent fractures on earth, the Babel principle splitting human community like an old pane of glass shattering into thousands of pieces: but it also recounts the determination and plan of God to reinvade earth from heaven, to reconnect earth to heaven, and therefore to remake that broken world. We come now to Act III, the New Creation, the new heavens and new earth, the new Jerusalem.

Reemphasizing a neglected truth

My aim in this chapter is to bring a neglected Christian truth back into the forefront of our thinking, and by so doing to inspire us with the majesty of where the ordinary local church is heading. Recently we celebrated my father's ninetieth birthday and had a photographer to record the occasion. A photographer needs to be a bit bossy to get the family group in order. Sometimes someone very important has got lost at the back, perhaps a much-loved granny hidden behind a tall grandson, and the photographer has to say, 'Granny, you are too important to be scarcely visible at the back; come and sit at the front.' In the same way, the doctrine of this chapter is a senior doctrine in the Christian family photograph, but has sometimes got a bit lost at the back. It is the doctrine we affirm whenever we say in the Apostles' Creed, 'I believe in the resurrection *of the body*.'

The glory of God spoiled on earth now

Before we think about the reunification of heaven and earth, it is helpful to consider what is going on, on earth now and in heaven now, before reunification, rather as a book about contemporary Germany would need to cover both East Germany and West Germany in order to understand the meaning of reunification. We begin with earth now.

The most important reason we need to study the doctrine of the New Creation is the glory of God. Earth is under rebel rule. It is governed, in a sense, by the prince of this world; cut adrift from the good government of God through obedient human beings, it is a mess of conflicting power structures. There are spiritual forces of evil expressing themselves in political oppression, in injustice, in personal slaveries to addictions, resentments, unforgiveness, greed and self-aggrandizement.

Because it is under a disordered rule, it gathers to itself its own glory. When the devil offers Jesus in the temptations, 'the kingdoms of the world and their glory', he is offering him stolen goods (Matt. 4:8). The whole creation is to be the theatre of God's glory. Whenever a human being, a family, a society, a government or a human project takes to itself glory, when I say, 'Well done me!', you say 'Well done you!', or we say 'Well done us!', we steal what is properly God's alone. When we speak of a 'Nature' programme, with no reference to the creator, this is a thieving of the glory of God.

A fractured earth governed by fighting ambitious human beings is not the theatre of God's glory as it ought to be. It is like a stage obscured by dry ice swirling around. In heaven there is glory; but on earth only echoes and footprints. A beautiful world has become a beautiful ruin.

So the question that ought to concern us is this: what happens to the glory of God? The creator God embarked on this project of making a good, very good, heavens and earth as the theatre of his glory: so what happens now? Is he to be frustrated by evil? Is his project to be finally spoiled, as a toy model might be ruined by a spiteful brother, spoiled and broken so it cannot be repaired and has to be thrown away with sadness? Or a beautiful garden graffitied and vandalized beyond repair, so it has to be completely abandoned, and the gardener has to start somewhere else in defeat? Is that what happens to the glory of God? That is the big question.

The answer is God wins, God remakes his broken world, and all the glory goes to God alone. The boy will rebuild his broken model; the gardener will restore his vandalized garden; the creator will remake his broken world.

Who is in heaven now?

If earth is spoiled, what is going on in heaven, God's 'space' as opposed to our 'space'? The New Testament teaches us at least four answers to the question, 'Who is in heaven now?'

God the Father is there. He is 'your Father, who is in heaven', 'your heavenly Father'. His will is done perfectly there ('as it is in heaven'). From there he has perfect knowledge of what happens on earth ('Your Father, who sees in secret' and 'knows what you need'). It is true there are 'spiritual forces of evil in the heavenly realms', but above them, at a higher level of authority, there is a space in which the Father's will is perfectly done: it is the throne room of the universe.[62]

Second, since the Ascension, Jesus Christ is in heaven, in his resurrection body. He has 'ascended to the Father', 'gone into heaven', 'entered into heaven itself', where he has 'sat down at the right hand of God'; and there at the Father's right hand he rules with 'all authority . . . in heaven and on earth'.[63] We cannot understand how he can be there in bodily form, in a 'place' that is inaccessible to our space-time universe, but it is important he is.

The bodily presence of Jesus in heaven shows us heaven does not mean a non-material place ('spiritual' in the Greek sense of immaterial). This idea comes from ancient Greek philosophical dualism, that opposes the world of matter and material with the world of 'spirit'. This kind of unbiblical thinking keeps rearing its ugly head. For example, in Eckhart Tolle's very popular New Age book *A New Earth* he has a page headed 'A new heaven and a new earth' in which he writes,

> The inspiration for the title of this book came from a Bible prophecy that seems more applicable now than at any other time in human history. It occurs in both the Old and the New Testament and speaks of the collapse of the existing world order and the arising of 'a new heaven and a new earth.' We need to understand here that heaven is not a location but refers to the inner realm of consciousness. This is the esoteric meaning of the word, and this is also its meaning in the teachings of Jesus. Earth, on the other hand, is the outer manifestation in form, which is always a reflection of the inner. Collective human consciousness and life on our planet are intrinsically connected. 'A new heaven' is the emergence of a transformed state of human consciousness, and 'a new earth' is its reflection in the physical realm.[64]

This is completely wrong! Heaven is a location. It is not a location within our space-time universe, but it is a location, a place other than our individual or collective consciousness. It is not found by going inside ourselves, but by belonging to Jesus who lives there in his resurrection body.

Third, it would seem dead Christians are there in spirit. They are spoken of as being 'asleep' (rather as Jesus described Lazarus as being 'asleep'), which seems to be a way of telling us their state is temporary, rather than telling us whether or not they are conscious; the New Testament is more interested in telling us about their future (bodily resurrection, when they 'awake') than in the precise details of their present state. It is enough they are with Jesus: they are 'with me where I am'. They are 'with Christ, which is far better'. They are with Jesus, like the penitent thief on the cross, now 'in paradise' (which would seem here to mean the place where the spirits of dead believers live temporarily with Jesus). There are 'many rooms' in the Father's house, and believers are assured of a home there. They are not there in body (for their bodies are rotting or have been cremated or destroyed); but they are there in spirit. So it is true when we die we go to heaven, in spirit but not in body, and temporarily, not forever.[65]

Finally, living Christians are there in status. Their citizenship is in heaven: this is where they now belong. In this sense they are 'seated with Christ in heavenly places'. So although they live on earth, here they are 'sojourners and exiles', 'exiles in dispersion here on earth'. The treasure or inheritance of living Christians is kept safely in heaven. They have 'treasures in heaven', 'an inheritance ... kept in heaven'. 'Every spiritual blessing' is theirs 'in heavenly places'. And the Holy Spirit on earth is 'the guarantee of our inheritance until we acquire possession of it'. Heaven is like the safe in which our treasure and inheritance is guarded. And the Holy Spirit like the title deed or deed of ownership of that inheritance.[66]

Heaven is not the end of the story

From time to time I take a very short train journey from Wimbledon in south-west London in to Waterloo, one of the central London termini. The journey lasts less than twenty minutes. Sometimes the following announcement is made over the intercom: 'Thank you for travelling with South West Trains. We are now approaching Waterloo, *which is our final destination.*' It feels to me a little over the top somehow, almost apocalyptic, this talk of 'final destinations'. But it also seems a bit sad. I look around at my fellow passengers and hope the station is not their final destination. I hope they are travelling on somewhere more interesting!

Heaven is not the final destination of Christian believers. It is a wonderful place, because it is with Jesus, which is far, far better than the troubles of this age (and a great deal better than Waterloo station). But it is not the end of the story. In fact, the New Testament is much more interested in what lies beyond heaven, than with heaven itself. It is true 'our citizenship is in heaven' and our 'inheritance that can never perish, spoil or fade' is 'kept in heaven for' us (1 Pet. 1:4,5). But we do not expect to enjoy that inheritance in heaven. Rather, *from heaven* 'we eagerly await a Saviour . . . the Lord Jesus Christ, who, by the power that enables him to bring everything under his control, will transform our lowly bodies so that they will be like his glorious body' (Phil. 3:20). We expect Jesus to come from heaven bringing our promised inheritance with him to earth. Again, when Paul writes to the church in Philippi he is confident God will carry on until he has finished his work in the church, he expects God to finish that work, not when they die and go to heaven, but at 'the day of Christ Jesus', which means the day of his return and the bodily resurrection (1:6). Paul is not longing finally to go to heaven, wonderful though that will be: he is reaching forwards to 'the resurrection from the dead', which means the resurrection of the *body* (3:11).

In the beatitudes from the Sermon on the Mount, Jesus promises those who are persecuted for his sake will have a great reward 'in *heaven*', but equally the meek 'will inherit the *earth*' (Matt. 5:5,12). He is not making separate promises in the beatitudes, as if those who pass the meekness test will be given the earth while those who are persecuted will go to heaven (and what happens to those who qualify on both counts?). Rather, he is giving the blessings that go with all the qualities of real godliness and genuine discipleship. There will be no difference between a reward in heaven and inheriting the earth, for the deep and simple reason that on that great day heaven and earth will be recombined!

In the apocalyptic language of Revelation, the souls of the martyrs do not say, 'Well, this is nice; now we're in heaven, so that's OK'; no, they call out 'in a loud voice, "How long, Sovereign Lord, holy and true, until you judge the inhabitants of the earth and avenge our blood?"' (Rev. 6:10). That is to say, they have a forward focus, longing for the final judgment and the resurrection of the dead.

This forward longing has been expressed in Christian history on gravestones and memorial tablets. For example, in the church of St Andrew the Great in Cambridge there is a memorial to two boys who died aged eleven and twelve. It describes them as having died, 'in hope of a blessed resurrection'. I came across an even more vivid example in Poets' Corner in Westminster Abbey, a place where a number of famous literary figures are buried. I was looking around feeling rather gloomy at the memorials to some notorious unbelievers like Oscar Wilde, when I stumbled upon this, to the sixteenth century poet Edmund Spencer:

HEARE LYES (EXPECTING THE SECOND COMMINGE OF OUR SAVIOVR CHRIST JESUS) THE BODY OF EDMOND SPENCER THE PRINCE OF POETS IN HIS TYME WHOSE DIVINE SPIRRIT NEEDS NOE OTHIR WITNESSE THEN THE WORKS WHICH HE LEFT BEHINDE HIM. HE WAS BORNE IN LONDON IN THE YEARE 1553 AND DIED IN THE YEARE 1598.

I nearly danced around the Abbey singing hallelujah! Here was one poet, at least, who died looking forward to that great day, the second coming of our saviour Christ Jesus. This is authentic Christian hope. This is why we pray the corporate prayer, 'Your kingdom come' in the Lord's Prayer, rather than the individual prayer, 'Please take me to heaven.'

Even Jesus Christ is looking forward to that great day. The letter to the Hebrews tells us that after the cross, Jesus 'sat down at the right hand of God'. But he did not sit down and relax, if we may put it reverently. No, 'Since that time he *waits* for his enemies to be made his footstool . . .' (Heb. 10:12,13). Even Jesus in heaven waits for the day when heaven can be reunited with earth. His kingdom may not be 'of this world' but is 'from another place' (i.e. it does not derive its authority from this fallen world but from the Father in heaven); nevertheless, his kingdom will be *over* this world, as we shall see (John 18:36).

So we must consider the hope for which living Christians wait, dead Christians wait, and even Jesus waits. This is why the New Testament speaks primarily not of two places (earth here and heaven above) but of two ages, of 'this age or the age to come', of 'the close of the age' (that is, of this age) or 'the end of the age', after which 'the righteous will shine like the sun in the kingdom of their Father'.[67] The Father will rule his kingdom not in heaven alone, but in the whole universe, over a reunited heavens and earth. The letter to the Hebrews speaks of 'the world to come' which will finally be under human rule, as it was always meant to be. It also speaks of 'the powers of the age to come' (Heb. 2:5; 6:5; Ps. 8). The expression 'eternal life' in John's gospel is probably best understood to mean, 'the life of the age to come', which means life in relationship with the Father and the Son (John 17:3). Jesus spoke of the 'renewal of all things' (literally, 'the regeneration'), which is the new birth of the whole cosmos (Matt. 19:28).

All this means we may need to reinterpret some of the language we use when we speak of heaven. We need to remember heaven sometimes serves as a shorthand for 'the New Creation'. There is a rousing popular song in which we sing, 'There's a place where the streets shine with the glory of the Lamb. There's a way; we can go there; we can live there beyond time' (extract taken from the song 'Because of You' by Paul Oakley. Copyright © 1986 Thankyou Music). Strictly speaking, I think we ought to sing, 'There's a place where the streets shine with the glory of the Lamb. But we won't go there; it will come to us!'

The New Jerusalem

In his letter to the Galatians Paul speaks of 'the Jerusalem that is above' who is the spiritual 'mother' of Christians; and the writer to the Hebrews says we 'have come to Mount Zion, to the heavenly Jerusalem, the city of the living God' (Gal. 4:26; Heb. 12:22). This new or heavenly Jerusalem is the spiritual reality to which the Old Testament Jerusalem pointed and which the local church anticipates. We should therefore expect it to express the realization (the 'making real or concrete') of the gathering of God. It does this in two ways.

First, it is the final gathering of all the people of God of every age. John describes a visionary anticipation of this in his famous words,

> After this I looked and there before me was a great multitude that no-one could count, from every nation, tribe, people and language, standing before the throne and in front of the Lamb. (Rev. 7:9)

This is the gathering anticipated on the first Christian Pentecost, where Babel began to be reversed and where the scattered human race began to be remade. Now at last it will be consummated forever and it will happen because they are gathered 'before the throne (of God) and in front of the Lamb.' As Paul says, the Christian hope is 'the coming of our Lord Jesus Christ *and our being gathered to him*' (2 Thess. 2:1). We are gathered to one another because – and only because – we are gathered to Jesus.

Second, it will also represent the regathering or reconnection of heaven and earth. When John finally sees the new Jerusalem at the end of Revelation, he sees it 'coming down out of heaven from God' (21:2,10). The great section from Revelation 21:1 through to Revelation 22:5 describes this beautiful city as the Bride of Christ, as the place where God lives with his people forever (so there is no need for a Temple). This is the time when the garden of Eden reoccupies the earth, so that the tree of life is there. This is when Eden is restored to the whole earth. The city is about the size of the entire known world;[68] this would seem to symbolize that this wonderful city extends throughout the New Creation. To be in the new heavens and the new earth is to be in the New Jerusalem, or at least to have free access in and out of its gates (Rev. 21:25).

When we try to understand this New Creation, we need to be very careful to be guided by what we are told in the New Testament, and to resist the temptation to try to tie up all the loose ends and answer all our questions. But I think we may make five clear statements about the New Creation, as follows.

1. The New Creation is real and physical

There is significant continuity between the present age and the New Creation of the age to come. The New

Creation is a 'spiritual' place populated by 'spiritual' bodies. But this does not mean it is immaterial. When Paul speaks of the resurrection body as being a 'spiritual body', he means a body patterned on the resurrection body of Jesus (1 Cor. 15:44). This was a physical body, one that could eat, be seen and touched (Luke 24:36–43). No doubt Jesus had a transformed physicality (he could come through a closed door, for example), but he was not ethereal, vague, immaterial or floating around: he was and is real. His body was 'spiritual' because it belonged to the age of the Spirit and not to the present age of corruption and decay.

In Romans 8 Paul writes of the creation waiting 'in eager expectation'; it has been 'subjected to frustration', the miserable processes of death and decay. But it 'will be liberated from its bondage to decay' and be brought into 'freedom'. It is 'groaning'; but its groaning is not the misery of death throes, of knowing it will be cast upon the cosmic scrap heap. Rather, its groaning is 'as in the pains of childbirth': this pain will lead to a new birth, the regeneration of the cosmos, and great joy (8:18–22). Creation does not groan because it knows its time is short and it will soon be destroyed: it groans like a mother-to-be enduring labour pains; its pain is suffused with hope. This is because it is not going simply to be replaced by an entirely discontinuous and non-physical order. The creation does not watch as Christians die and are transferred to heaven, knowing that on the last day the final cohort of Christians will be transferred to heaven: and then the creation – or what is left of it – is doomed to destruction. Far from it: the creation longs to be set free from bondage. The creation is not a prisoner on death row, but a prisoner awaiting release. The voice John hears in Revelation 21 does not say, 'I make all new things', but 'I make all things new' (v. 5): we expect a regeneration not a simple replacement of this cosmos.

This ensures God wins. God made a good universe. That universe has been spoiled, but God has not given up on it: he does not say, 'Well, that was a pity; I'd better start again.' No, he will end the story with a good, real, physical cosmos that is the completion and perfection of his original creation. Nothing can stop him doing it.

The physical delight we may experience in the beauty of music, the stimulus of sport, the intimacy of sex within marriage, the taste of good food, the wonders of travel, all these will be there in transformed and transcended form in the New Creation. They will not be the same: for example, there will be no marriage. But all the good delights human beings experience will be transcended and exceeded in that new age. No believer who 'misses out' on any delight in this age will miss out for eternity; far from it.

2. Heaven and earth are reunited only at the cross

Atonement is the necessary ground of the New Creation. The most famous Old Testament prophecy of the New Creation is probably Isaiah 65:17–25, which begins, 'For behold, I create new heavens and a new earth . . .' But, strikingly, this New Creation centres and focuses on Jerusalem (v. 18). In fact, it is impossible to separate the New Creation from the new Jerusalem. That is, in the imagery of Old Covenant language, heaven is reunited with earth through the place of atonement, the place of sacrifice. The logic is simple. Why was heaven estranged from earth? Because of sin, guilt and the wrath of God. So how can heaven be reunited with earth? Through atonement. It is for this reason the crucified Lord is the only one in whom things in heaven and things on earth will be united (Eph. 1:10). The cross of Christ is the intersection of earth and heaven. It is the place on earth where God's space intersects with our space without destroying us utterly, because there the judgment fell on God.

3. The New Creation is ruled by Christ's people

In Romans 8 we read that creation 'waits in eager expectation for the sons of God to be revealed' and looks forward to being 'brought into the glorious freedom of the children of God' (vv.19,21). Here 'sons of God' does not just mean men: it means God's heirs, both men and women. But why is the future joy of creation so tied up with the children of God? The original purpose of God was for his good creation to be governed by a harmonious humanity. Creation is like a play in which the lead actors are drunk or absent, not playing their parts, or an orchestra in which the conductor is just having fun on his own behind the scenes. What creation needs is the sons and daughters of God redeemed, restored, transformed, to govern it with justice. Then the orchestra will sing God's praises, and the play be performed to God's honour. This is the idea C.S. Lewis used when he spoke of Narnia waiting for 'sons of Adam and daughters of Eve' to come and rule it. We do not yet see humankind governing the world as we ought, but we do see a human Jesus 'crowned with glory and honour' and this means one day Christian people will 'judge' (i.e. govern) the world (Heb. 2:6–9; 1 Cor. 6:2). The point Paul makes in 1 Corinthians 6:1–6 is if we are going to govern the world in the age to come, we really ought to be able to learn to live together in harmony in this age, in the local church!

4. The New Creation is purged of all rebellion

For Babel to be finally reversed, the New Creation needs to be radically purged of all sin. The passage that perhaps stresses most forcibly the discontinuity between this age and the age to come is 2 Peter 3:3–13. Here we read 'the present heavens and earth are reserved for fire, being kept for the day of judgment and destruction of ungodly men' and the 'heavens will disappear with a roar; the elements will be destroyed by fire, and the earth and everything in it will be laid bare' (vv. 7,10). The fires of judgment will have to burn very deep and will destroy, root and branch, all evildoers and sources of evil.

Even then, however, we must not misunderstand this as though Peter were simply teaching the replacement of this creation by an entirely discontinuous one. For Peter puts the fire of judgment in parallel with the waters of judgment in Noah's flood, under which the earth 'was deluged and destroyed' (2 Pet. 3:16). But the land then was not 'destroyed' in an absolute sense: after the flood, the Bible story did not start again on Mars! No, the flood represented deep cleansing rather than simple replacement. Just so with the New Creation: the new heavens and earth are not a parallel universe, but this universe purged and redeemed.

We must not minimize the depth of this necessary purging. It is terribly possible to be thrown into hell or the eternal fire. There will be a terrible storm of judgment that will destroy every life not built on hearing Jesus' words and doing them. There will be a deep and dreadful shaking and only the city with foundations will stand. It is possible finally to be excluded from the presence of the Lord, to be thrown into outer darkness, to be consigned to eternal weeping and regrets. The sexually immoral, idolaters, adulterers, homosexual practitioners, thieves, the greedy, drunkards, revilers and swindlers will not inherit the kingdom of God. The cowardly, the faithless, the detestable, murderers, sexually immoral, sorcerers, idolaters and all liars will be thrown into the lake that burns with fire, which is the second death.[69] The New Creation cannot be born without terrible radical suffering and exclusion and so the form of this world as it is in this age, is passing away; it will be rolled up like unwanted clothes.[70] Heaven and earth, in their rebellious corrupt form in this age, will pass away, as they did in the days of Noah: only Jesus' words and all that is built on that will last (Matt. 24:35).

5. Creation must be deeply transformed

This purging means the New Creation will be a deep transformation of this present age. I was preaching on this subject once and someone came up to me and asked, 'How will there be room on this earth for all the believers who have ever lived? I can't visualize it.' I think the New Testament gives us three answers to that sort of question.

1. Just as Jesus' resurrection body was real, physical and recognizable (the Jesus who rose was the same Jesus), and just as it was also transformed from weakness to glory, so the resurrection body will be deeply transformed, and the New Creation likewise will be deeply transformed.
2. When people asked Paul the same sort of question he said (in effect), 'Don't ask stupid questions!' He wanted his questioners to grasp how deeply this body must be transformed to be suited to that new age, just as a seed is deeply transformed when it becomes its plant or crop. Our resurrection bodies will be so astonishingly greater they will be to these mortal bodies like plants to their seeds, like oak trees

to acorns, or, as he puts it elsewhere, like a solid building to a fragile tent (1 Cor. 15:35,36; 2 Cor. 5:1–5).

3. When the Sadducees tried to trick Jesus with this, and they came up with a clever conundrum he replied, 'You are in error because you do not know the scriptures or the power of God.' (Matt. 22:23–33).

So there's no point asking, 'Where will London be? What about this planet? Will my dog be there?' These are foolish questions which reveal we have not grasped how deeply transformed the New Creation will be. It will be deeply and wonderfully transformed from the creation in this age. The New Creation will not be this creation trimmed with a few improved features added – as the pictures in the Jehovah's Witnesses magazine delivered to our door suggest – a world that is pretty much recognizable as this world but with a few 'tweaks', perhaps a lion lying down with a lamb here or there! The New Creation is unimaginably better, deeper, fuller, and more substantial, than this age. Every cell, every atom, and every molecule in the universe is corrupted and spoiled and not as it ought to be. The transformation necessary to root sin out of the universe is a root and branch matter.

So creation will be wonderfully and deeply transformed. We cannot achieve this by our human endeavours. No matter how well we do our politics, or measure up to our ecological responsibility (and we ought), we will never create the New Creation. It is the Sovereign work of God alone and all the glory will be his.

In thinking about the New Creation, we need to be careful to give proper weight to the twin emphases in Scripture of continuity and discontinuity. If we go too far in the direction of continuity, we slip into a human-centred optimism which almost thinks by our actions we can turn this age into the age to come. We think of a world rather like this one but a bit better, such that by some good human initiatives, a bit of luck and a following wind we might create it ourselves. That would be nonsense. How arrogant!

On the other hand, if we go too far in the direction of discontinuity, we slip into thinking of the New Creation as a kind of 'heaven' place which is a bit ghostly and insubstantial, and essentially a place that is entered by being taken out of this creation and beamed up by an interstellar teleporter like some kind of Christianized 'Star Trekker' into a different place. If we think like this we will be inclined not to see the value of our secular work or our responsibilities to care for the environment and to seek justice in the world.

Some Implications of the New Creation

The doctrine of the New Creation magnifies the church. It is a great antidote to western individualism, in which we regard the church as an aid to me in my discipleship, somewhere I go so that I may be encouraged. It is that (e.g. Heb. 10:24,25), but it is much more. It is the anticipation in this age of the new humanity who will rule the age to come. It is the human society in which barriers are broken by the cross, by justification through grace alone by faith alone, in which human pride is levelled, Babel undone, men and women gathered in Christ to be all one in Christ Jesus, to be the united humanity to rule the age to come, to inherit the earth. When we bring the New Creation to the front of the family photograph of Christian doctrines, we bring the doctrine of the church along with it.

This doctrine helps us think about Christian perseverance as a corporate thing. We are to endure to the end not only as individuals, but together. If we think when we die we have arrived at our final destination, I fear we have removed from Christian discipleship a deep corporate incentive for perseverance. That is to say, I will hope for the future. I will long to be with Christ. But it will be 'I' as an individual who long, because when I die, my longings will be fulfilled, my path will be at an end.

However, it is interesting the New Testament does not seem to encourage this. When in James 5 the Christians are suffering because of injustice and poverty, James does not say, 'Chin up, keep going, before long you will die and then it will all be alright for you (and let those who are still alive go hang).' No, he says, 'Be patient, then, brothers, until the Lord's coming . . . be patient and stand firm, because the Lord's coming is near . . . The Judge is standing at the door!' (Jas 5:7–9). Keep waiting, keep on keeping on, hold on, because we are all together waiting in hope. We wait, the Christian dead wait and cry, 'How long?', the whole creation waits, even Christ himself waits for that great day. So let us hold on as we wait together and persevere together. This truth sets before believers a pattern for perseverance.

Questions for Discussion

1. Review the chapter. What is God's plan for the end of time? How does this plan complete his glory?
2. In what ways will the New Creation be in continuity with this age, and in what ways will it be different?
3. What does the word 'spiritual' in a phrase like 'a spiritual body' mean in the New Testament, and how is this different from the popular use of the word 'spiritual'?

4. I have suggested talking about 'heaven' can mislead us into forgetting the wonderful fullness of the New Creation. Do you think this is true? If so, how can we change the way we speak, to keep the New Creation in the centre of our thinking?
5. What difference does the doctrine of the New Creation make to the way we relate to other Christians?
6. When the local church seems very ordinary and sometimes discouraging, how can we help one another remember where it is heading?

Conclusion

The Glory of the God Who is One

We began our Bible tour with the God who is One. We will end with this same great God. At the start we glimpsed one harmonious creation that was the theatre of his glory. But very soon we saw that peace shattered in every way, in the tragic journey from Eden to Babel. The Bible story of the remaking of a broken world is not primarily about your or my individual salvation. Nor even is it primarily about our shared destiny as the children of God in the New Creation. Supremely it is about the restored glory of God. It is about the whole creation singing again his praises in harmony, with no discordant voices.

The New Creation will resound to the glory of God and of Christ. The New Creation will be – even more deeply than the unspoiled creation at the beginning – the theatre of God's glory. Creation will be restored and God will win: it will be a living visible tribute to his glory. Because atonement is its ground and foundation, the Lord Jesus Christ will stand at its centre as the Lamb who was slain. Because by his death the Son of God ransomed people for God, broke the barriers, and created a new united redeemed humanity, gathered from every nation, the glory will be to God alone.

Now he waits for all things to be put under his feet. The Bible story is about every hostile power surrendering to Jesus who will make them a footstool for his feet, and it is about this Jesus handing back the whole created order to the Father, 'so that God may be all in all' (1 Cor. 15:24–28). And when God is again all in all the song of the New Creation can begin in earnest, to be sung ever fresh for all eternity.

This is the destiny of the local church; this is the wonderful consummation for which the local church is preparing. The glory of God for all eternity is bound up with what happens in local churches now. They are the concrete realization in this age of the peace-producing dynamics of the age to come. Let us commit ourselves to honouring God in the local church and praise God for every evidence we see in local churches that God is remaking a broken world. To him be the glory.

Endnotes

1   Nick Spencer, *Beyond Belief? Barriers and Bridges to Faith Today* (The London Institute for Contemporary Christianity, 2003), pp. 17, 54.

2   Vaughan Roberts, *God's Big Picture* (Leicester: IVP, 2002).

3   T. Desmond Alexander, *From Eden to the New Jerusalem* (Nottingham: IVP, 2008).

4   Gregory of Nazianzus, *Oration* 2, para.1 (362 AD).

5   Francis Schaeffer, *The God Who is There* (Downers Grove, Illinois: IVP, 1968).

6   *The Independent*, 12 April 1999.

7   Zech. 14:9, ESV. The ESV is more literal here than the NIV.

8   *The Guardian*, 23 December 2006.

9   All quoted in Meic Pearse, *The Gods of War: Is Religion the Primary Cause of Violent Conflict?* (Downers Grove, Illinois: IVP, 2007), pp. 13, 14.

10   Isa. 51:3; Joel 2:3; Ezek. 28:13; 36:33–35.

11   *Nature* 365 (7 October 1993), p. 484.

12   John Steinbeck, *East of Eden* (first published 1952; my edition London: Penguin Classics, 2000), pp. 303–306, 602.

13   The King James Version translates the Hebrew imperfect tense very literally; but it is clear that it has the force of a command, as in the Ten Commandments ('Thou shalt . . .').

14   *The Economist*, 8 March 2008.

15 Eckhart Tolle, *A New Earth: Awakening to Your Life's Purpose* (London: Penguin Books, 2006), especially pp. 20–26, 57.

16 Gen. 3:15; 4:3,4,15; 5:24; 7:13–16.

17 Alexander, *From Eden . . .* , p. 30.

18 *The Economist*, 14 March 2008, pp. 53, 56.

19 Robert Cooper, *The Breaking of Nations: Order and Chaos in the Twenty-first Century* (Boston: Atlantic Monthly Press, 2003).

20 Review in *The Economist*, 31 January 2009, p. 63f.

21 Guy Brandon, *Just Sex: Is It Ever Just Sex?* (Nottingham: IVP, 2009), p. 92.

22 Jorge Luis Borges, *The Library of Babel* (Boston: David R. Godine, 2000).

23 For this and many other fascinating uses of the Babel story in contemporary art, see I.L. Finkel and M.J. Seymour (eds) *Babylon: Myth and Reality* (London: the British Museum Press, 2008), pp. 203–208.

24 Quoted in Allister Sparks, *The Mind of South Africa: The Story of the Rise and Fall of Apartheid* (Johannesburg and Cape Town: Jonathan Ball publishers, 2003), p. 294.

25 Jonathan Sacks, *The Home We Build Together: Recreating Society* (London: Continuum, 2007) p. 3.

26 Otomo no Yakamochi.

27 The closing date is written as 1918/19 because although the Armistice was signed in 1918 the Treaty of Versailles was not signed until 1919. It is interesting to note a number of war memorials give 1914–19 as the dates.

28 Quoted in Lesslie Newbigin, *The Light Has Come* (Grand Rapids, Michigan: Eerdmans, 1982), p. 160.

29 Francis Fukuyama, *The End of History and the Last Man* (London: Penguin, 1993), p. 233.

30 Michael Jensen, 'Fraternity', in *Churchman* 122/4 (Winter 2008), pp. 331–334.

31 Liam Goligher, *Joseph: The Hidden Hand of God* (Fearn, Ross-shire: Christian Focus, 2008), p. 179.

[32] The KJV calls it 'the church in the wilderness'.

[33] See, e.g., Josh. 24, 1 Sam. 7:5 and Neh. 8.

[34] Edmund Gosse, *Father and Son* (London: Penguin, 1989), p. 39.

[35] 1 Kings 19:12, translated 'a gentle whisper' in NIV. No-one knows the precise meaning of this word, and it certainly doesn't mean that we discern God's voice purely subjectively, as is sometimes suggested.

[36] C.S. Lewis, *A Grief Observed* (London: Faber, 1966), pp. 18, 19.

[37] Naomi Klein, *No Logo* (Toronto: Knopf Canada, 2000), p. 345.

[38] A fuller treatment of what follows is found in Alexander, *From Eden . . .*, pp. 31–60.

[39] For example, 1 Chr. 28:2 or Ps. 132:7 (another of the Psalms of Ascent).

[40] Alexander, *From Eden . . .*, pp. 20–23.

[41] Gen. 3:8; Lev. 26:12; Deut. 23:14; 2 Sam. 7:6,7.

[42] Gen. 3:24; Exod. 25:18–22; 26:31; 36:35; 1 Kgs 6:23–29; 2 Chr. 3:14.

[43] Ps. 68:26. See also Ps. 22:25; 26:12; 35:18; 40:9,10.

[44] E.g. 1 Sam. 11:11; 28:4; 2 Sam. 10:17.

[45] E.g. Num. 10:35,36; Ps. 68:1,14,30; 89:10; 92:9; 144:6; Isa. 33:3; Jer. 49:5,32,36; Nah. 3:18.

[46] 1 Sam. 16 – 2 Sam. 5. On this, see John Woodhouse's excellent study, *Looking for a Leader* (Wheaton, Illinois: Crossway Books, 2008).

[47] 1 Kgs 11:37,38; 12:26–33; 13:33,34.

[48] Ezek. 20:23,24; and see also 22:15; 12:12–14; 17:21.

[49] See p. 7 on Ps. 122:1-5.

[50] Kenneth Anger, *Hollywood Babylon* (New York: Dell Publishing, 1975).

[51] C.S. Lewis, *The Great Divorce* (Glasgow: Collins, 1977), p. 19.

[52] See the books of Ezra and Nehemiah. Also, e.g. Ezra 3:1; 7:28; 8:15; 9:4; 10:1; Neh. 5:16.

53   Isa. 11:12; 27:12; 40:11; 43:5; 49:5; 54:7; 56:8; 60:4; 66:18.

54   Jer. 23:3; 29:14; 31:8,10; 32:37.

55   Ezek. 11:16,17; 28:25; 34:12,13; 36:19,24; 37:21; 39:27,28.

56   One of the very best is John Stott, *The Cross of Christ* (Leicester: IVP, 1986).

57   Two recent helpful books are Graham Beynon, *God's New Community: New Testament Patterns for Today's Church* (Nottingham: IVP, 2005) and Melvin Tinker and Nathan Buttery, *Body Beautiful: Recovering the Biblical View of the Church* (Milton Keynes: Authentic Media, 2003).

58   Matt. 20:1–16, the parable of the labourers in the vineyard.

59   *The Economist*, 18 October 2008, p. 82.

60   Acts 4:27; see also Matt. 26:3,57; 27:62; Luke 22:66.

61   The former, for example, in Iconium in Acts 14:19, or Thessalonica in Acts 17:5. The latter can be seen, for example, in Cyprus in Acts 13:6-11, or in Ephesus in Acts 19:23–41.

62   Matt. 5:45,48; 6:1–9; 10:32,33; 23:9; Eph. 6:12.

63   John 20:17; 1 Pet. 3:22; Heb. 9:24; 10:12,13; Matt. 28:18.

64   Tolle, *A New Earth*, p. 23.

65   1 Thess. 4:13; John 11:11; 17:24; Phil. 1:21,23; John 14:2.

66   Phil. 3:20; Eph. 2:6; 1 Pet. 1:1; 2:11; Matt. 6:20; 19:21; 1 Pet. 1:4; Eph. 1:3,11–14.

67   Matt. 12:32; Eph. 1:21; Matt. 13:40,49; 24:3; 28:20; 13:43.

68   G.K. Beale, *The Book of Revelation* (Grand Rapids: Eerdmans, 1999), on Rev. 21:16.

69   Matt. 5:29,30; 18:8,9; 7:24–27; Heb. 12:26-28; 2 Thess. 1:7; Matt. 8:12; 13:49,50; 1 Cor. 6:9,10; Rev. 21:8.

70   1 Cor. 7:31; Heb. 1:11, quoting Ps. 102.

Acknowledgments

In an aside at a conference, I once suggested that it would be possible to do a Bible overview themed around scattering and gathering. I had been mulling on this idea for years, ever since doing a Bible study on the words "scatter" and "gather" about thirty years ago. Then Jonathan Carswell persuaded me to write the overview, and here it is. I'm grateful to him for his encouragement. I'm also grateful to Brian Elphick for allowing me to try some of the material at the St Andrew the Great student house-parties in March 2009 and to Jonathan Fletcher for his invitation to preach some more of it at Emmanuel, Wimbledon in April and May 2009. Others have made helpful comments, including my wife Carolyn, my friend Jason Fletcher, and my colleagues Tim McMahon, Stuart Allen, Christine Mulryne and Nikki Boniface at the Cornhill Training Course. I owe thanks to them all, and also to Zoë Moore for her careful editing work on the original manuscript.

Index of Biblical References

Genesis

Gen. 1:1	8
Gen. 1:1 – 2:3	5
Gen. 1:26–28	6
Gen. 2:4–25	5
Gen. 2:9	70
Gen. 2:10	70
Gen. 2:16,17	9
Gen. 2:17	13
Gen. 2:18	7
Gen. 3 – 10	10
Gen. 3:4	16
Gen. 3:5	9
Gen. 3:8	6,10,70
Gen. 3:12,13	10
Gen. 3:15	17
Gen. 3:22	23,70
Gen. 3:24	2,63,70
Gen. 4:1–16	11
Gen. 4:3,4	17
Gen. 4:10	144
Gen. 4:15	17
Gen. 4:16	2
Gen. 4:18–24	12
Gen. 4:24	159
Gen. 5:24	17
Gen. 6:11	13
Gen. 7:13–16	17
Gen. 9:18–27	29
Gen. 10:5	19
Gen. 10:25	19
Gen. 11:1–9	18,19,20
Gen. 11:5	47
Gen. 12 – 50	44
Gen. 12:1–3	42
Gen. 15:5	43
Gen. 17:5–8	43
Gen. 22:1–19	69
Gen. 22:17	43
Gen. 22:18	43
Gen. 28:3	43,108
Gen. 28:10–22	69
Gen. 35:11	43,108
Gen. 48:4	43,108

Exodus

Exod. 1 – 15	45
Exod. 1:1–5	45
Exod. 1:6,7	45
Exod. 3:12	46
Exod. 6:7	xiv
Exod. 12:37,38	45
Exod. 13 – 18	45
Exod. 18:13–18	45
Exod. 19:20	47
Exod. 20:1–17	53,54
Exod. 24:6–9	144
Exod. 25 – 40	70
Exod. 25:18–22	70
Exod. 25:31–35	70
Exod. 26:31	70
Exod. 32:1	55,162
Exod. 36:35	70

Leviticus

Lev. 19:18	54
Lev. 23:4	68
Lev. 26:12	70

Numbers

Num. 10:11 – 36:13	66
Num. 10:35,36	76
Num. 16:11	165

Deuteronomy

Deut. 1:1	49
Deut. 1:9–12	46
Deut. 1:19 – 3:29	66
Deut. 4:10	47,50
Deut. 4:10–15	51
Deut. 4:13	52
Deut. 4:14	52
Deut. 4:15–19	55
Deut. 4:24	63
Deut. 4:25–27	89
Deut. 4:25–28	61
Deut. 4:30,31	64
Deut. 5:1	49
Deut. 5:6–21	53
Deut. 5:12–15	53
Deut. 6:4	xiv,xviii
Deut. 9:10	48,52
Deut. 10:4	48
Deut. 10:5	52
Deut. 18:16	48
Deut. 21:22,23	119
Deut. 23:2–4	48
Deut. 23:14	70
Deut. 28:15	89
Deut. 28:25	89
Deut. 28:64	89
Deut. 31:1	49
Deut. 31:11	49

Joshua

Josh. 13 – 21	74
Josh. 24	48

Judges

Judg. 6:15	74
Judg. 8:1	74
Judg. 11:1	74
Judg. 12:1	74
Judg. 17–21	77
Judg. 17:6	77

Judg. 18:1	77	
Judg. 19:1	77	
Judg. 20,21	74	
Judg. 21:25	77	

1 Samuel

1 Sam. 2:8	xvii	
1 Sam. 7:5	48	
1 Sam. 11:11	76	
1 Sam. 16 – 2 Sam. 5	77	
1 Sam. 16:1–13	76	
1 Sam. 28:4	76	

2 Samuel

2 Sam. 5:6–10	67,77
2 Sam. 7:5–16	78
2 Sam. 7:6,7	70
2 Sam. 10:17	76

1 Kings

1 Kgs 5 – 8	69
1 Kgs 5:13–16	86
1 Kgs 6:23–29	70
1 Kgs 11:1–43	86
1 Kgs 11:29–36	87
1 Kgs 11:37,38	88
1 Kgs 12	87
1 Kgs 12:26–33	88
1 Kgs 13:33,34	88
1 Kgs 19:12	59

2 Kings

2 Kgs 17:1–6	88
2 Kgs 17:7–41	88
2 Kgs 17:21	87
2 Kgs 18 – 19	73
2 Kgs 18 – 25	88
2 Kgs 24,25	88

1 Chronicles

1 Chr. 13:5	49
1 Chr. 16:35	76
1 Chr. 28:2	69

2 Chronicles

2 Chr. 3:1	69
2 Chr. 3:14	70
2 Chr. 36:22,23	96

Ezra

Ezra 3:1	97
Ezra 7:28	97
Ezra 8:15	97
Ezra 9:4	97
Ezra 10:1	97

Nehemiah

Neh. 1:8,9	97
Neh. 5:16	97
Neh. 8	48,97
Neh. 8:1–8	97

Esther

Esth. 3:8	99

Psalms

Ps. 2:2	165
Ps. 8	182
Ps. 22:25	75
Ps. 26:12	75

Ps. 35:18	75
Ps. 40:9,10	75
Ps. 44:11	90
Ps. 47:2	xviii
Ps. 47:9	43
Ps. 48:2	72
Ps. 48:8	72
Ps. 50:5	47
Ps. 68:1	76
Ps. 68:14	76
Ps. 68:30	76
Ps. 68:26	75
Ps. 84:1,2	71
Ps. 84:7	71
Ps. 89:10	76
Ps. 92:9	76
Ps. 102	189
Ps. 106:24–27	90
Ps. 106:47	99
Ps. 120	68,83,108
Ps. 121	68
Ps. 122	67,68,69,98
Ps. 122:3	71
Ps. 122:5	75
Ps. 125:1	72
Ps. 125:2	68
Ps. 132:7	69
Ps. 137	92
Ps. 144:6	76

Ecclesiastes

Eccl. 5:2	xix

Isaiah

Isa. 1:13	163
Isa. 2:1–4	80
Isa. 5:7	78
Isa. 10:13,14	30
Isa. 11:12	100
Isa. 13:11	93
Isa. 14:4–6	93
Isa. 14:13	94
Isa. 27:12	100
Isa. 33:3	76
Isa. 40:11	100
Isa. 43:5	100
Isa. 47:8	94
Isa. 49:5	100
Isa. 51:3	6
Isa. 52:13 – 53:12	117
Isa. 53:6	25
Isa. 54:7	100
Isa. 56:8	100
Isa. 60:4	100
Isa. 65:17–25	186
Isa. 66:18	100

Jeremiah

Jer. 9:13–16	90
Jer. 10:21	90
Jer. 13:24	90
Jer. 18:17	91
Jer. 23:1,2	91
Jer. 23:3	100
Jer. 29:14	100
Jer. 31:8,10	100
Jer. 32:37	100
Jer. 49:5	76

Jer. 49:32   76
Jer. 49:36   76

Lamentations
Lam. 4:16   91

Ezekiel
Ezek. 11:16,17   101
Ezek. 12:12–14   91
Ezek. 17:21   91
Ezek. 20:23,24   91
Ezek. 22:15   91
Ezek. 28:13   6
Ezek. 28:25   101
Ezek. 34 – 37   123,174
Ezek. 34:5   78
Ezek. 34:12,13   101
Ezek. 36:19,24   101
Ezek. 36:28   xiv
Ezek. 36:33–35   6
Ezek. 37:1–14   124
Ezek. 37:21   101
Ezek. 39:27,28   101
Ezek. 47:1–12   70

Daniel
Dan. 4:29–33   31

Hosea
Hos. 1:1–9   88
Hos. 1:10,11   101
Hos. 2:14–23   101

Joel
Joel 2:3   6

Amos
Amos 5:21   163

Micah
Mic. 2:12   101
Mic. 4:1–3   80
Mic. 4:6   101

Nahum
Nah. 3:18   76

Zephaniah
Zeph. 3:10,19,20   102

Haggai
Hag. 1:1   99
Hag. 2:3   98

Zechariah
Zech. 1:19   89
Zech. 7:13,14   91
Zech. 10:8,9   102
Zech. 14:9   xviii

Matthew
Matt. 1:1–17   110
Matt. 1:12   99
Matt. 3:11   127
Matt. 3:12   111
Matt. 4:8   176
Matt. 4:18–22   111
Matt. 4:23 – 5:1   112
Matt. 5:5,12   180
Matt. 5:29,30   189
Matt. 5:45,48   177

Matt. 6	150	Matt. 23:9	177
Matt. 6:1–9	177	Matt. 23:27	119
Matt. 6:10	xix	Matt. 23:37	114
Matt. 6:20	179	Matt. 24:3	182
Matt. 7:24–27	189	Matt. 24:31	113
Matt. 8:1–4	112	Matt. 24:35	189
Matt. 8:10–12	118	Matt. 26:3,57	165
Matt. 8:11,12	116	Matt. 26:31	140
Matt. 8:12	119,189	Matt. 27:33	xxi
Matt. 8:16,17	116	Matt. 27:62	165
Matt. 9:9–11	112	Matt. 28:18	121,177
Matt. 9:9–13	115	Matt. 28:20	182
Matt. 9:35–38	113		
Matt. 9:36	78	**Mark**	
Matt. 10:32,33	177	Mark 3:6	165
Matt. 10:34–39	114	Mark 8:31	117
Matt. 11:19	112	Mark 9:31	117
Matt. 12:6	81	Mark 10:33,34	117
Matt. 12:30	113	Mark 12:13	165
Matt. 12:32	182	Mark 14:50	139
Matt. 13:40,49	182	Mark 15:22	107
Matt. 13:43	182		
Matt. 13:49,50	189	**Luke**	
Matt. 16:18	113,146	Luke 1:51	24
Matt. 18	149,157	Luke 1:51–55	109
Matt. 18:1	146	Luke 2:25–35	108
Matt. 18:8,9	189	Luke 2:29–32	109
Matt. 18:21–35	157	Luke 7:11–17	112
Matt. 19:21	179	Luke 12:49–53	114
Matt. 19:28	183	Luke 14:15–24	114
Matt. 20:1–16	159	Luke 15:1	112
Matt. 21:31	151	Luke 15:11–24	164
Matt. 22:1–14	114	Luke 19:9	112
Matt. 22:23–33	190	Luke 22:66	165
Matt. 23	150	Luke 23:12	165

Luke 23:43 145
Luke 24:36–43 185

John
John 1:11–13 133
John 1:14 82
John 1:29–34 127
John 1:46 148
John 2:19–22 82
John 3:1–8 134
John 7:39 128
John 7:42 148
John 9:1,2 113
John 10:14–16 113
John 10:16 155
John 11:11 179
John 11:49–50 117
John 11:51–52 118
John 12:32 118,140
John 14:2 179
John 14:15–23 135
John 16:32 140
John 17:3 183
John 17:24 179
John 17:20–23 136
John 18:36 160,182
John 20:17 177

Acts
Acts 1:4,5 129
Acts 1:12–26 129
Acts 2 42
Acts 2:1–12 130
Acts 2:38,39 131
Acts 3:25 131

Acts 4:5–6 166
Acts 4:27 165
Acts 7:38 47,141
Acts 8:1 140
Acts 10 132
Acts 11:19–21 141
Acts 11:20 152
Acts 13:6–11 166
Acts 14:19 166
Acts 17:5 166
Acts 19:23–41 166

Romans
Rom. 1:5 121
Rom. 1:23–25 58
Rom. 3:21–26 146
Rom. 4:13 44,128
Rom. 5:1 120
Rom. 5:1–11 145
Rom. 5:10,11 120
Rom. 5:12 14
Rom. 8:18–22 185
Rom. 8:19,21 187
Rom. 12:21 160
Rom. 16:26 121

1 Corinthians
1 Cor. 1:2 155
1 Cor. 3:9,16 141
1 Cor. 3:16 82
1 Cor. 5:4 141
1 Cor. 6:2 187
1 Cor. 6:9,10 189
1 Cor. 6:19 82
1 Cor. 7:31 189

1 Cor. 8:4	xv
1 Cor. 8:6	xiv
1 Cor. 12:4–6	132
1 Cor. 14:33	132
1 Cor. 15:24–28	196
1 Cor. 15:35,36	190
1 Cor. 15:44185	

2 Corinthians

2 Cor. 1:20	110
2 Cor. 5:1–5	190
2 Cor. 5:21	120
2 Cor. 6:16	82

Galatians

Gal. 2:11–16	153
Gal. 3:8	42
Gal. 3:13	120
Gal. 3:13,14	128
Gal. 3:16	42
Gal. 3:29	42
Gal. 4:25	81
Gal. 4:26	183

Ephesians

Eph. 1:3	179
Eph. 1:9,10	173
Eph. 1:10	186
Eph. 1:11–14	179
Eph. 1:21	182
Eph. 2:6	179
Eph. 2:14–18	152
Eph. 2:21,22	82
Eph. 4:3–6	133
Eph. 4:12,13	133

Eph. 4:28	54
Eph. 5:5	58
Eph. 6:2	54
Eph. 6:12	177

Philippians

Phil. 1:6	180
Phil. 1:21,23	179
Phil. 2:6–11	121
Phil. 2:8	148
Phil. 3:11	180
Phil. 3:20	179,180

Colossians

Col. 3:5	58
Col. 3:12,13	157

1 Thessalonians

1 Thess. 2:14	155
1 Thess. 4:13	179

2 Thessalonians

2 Thess. 1:7	189
2 Thess. 2:1	184

1 Timothy

1 Tim. 6:17	54

2 Timothy

2 Tim. 3:5	163

Hebrews

Heb. 1:11	189
Heb. 2:5	182
Heb. 2:6–9	187

Heb. 6:5	182	**2 Peter**	
Heb. 9:24	177	2 Pet. 3:3–13	188
Heb. 10:12,13	177,182	2 Pet. 3:16	188
Heb. 10:24,25	191		
Heb. 10:25	142	**1 John**	
Heb. 12:18	64	1 John 5:21	58
Heb. 12:18–21	63		
Heb. 12:18–29	142	**Revelation**	
Heb. 12:22	66,80,82,183	Rev. 6:10	181
Heb. 12:22–24	143	Rev. 7:9	43,183
Heb. 12:26–28	189	Rev. 21:2	83
Heb. 12:29	63	Rev. 21:2,10	184
Heb. 13:5	54,156	Rev. 21:5	185
		Rev. 21:8	189
James		Rev. 21:25	184
Jas 2:2	141		
Jas 2:13	159		
Jas 4:1–3	155		
Jas 4:4–10	156		
Jas 5:7–9	192		
1 Peter			
1 Pet. 1:1	177,179		
1 Pet. 1:4	179		
1 Pet. 1:4,5	180		
1 Pet. 2:11	177,179		
1 Pet. 2:5	82,141		
1 Pet. 2:23	160,161		
1 Pet. 3:18	144		
1 Pet. 3:22	177		
1 Pet. 5:9	155		